One Saturday morning in the spring of 1985, I attended a business presentation meeting. I felt as if I had been struck by lightning. I decided to make a change in my life. I wanted to become successful. I began looking for the miracle at the end of the road. I found out that miracles happen every step of the way.

PRESS

www.worldsystembuilder.com

Building
PEOPLE

The Journey of a Builder

2.0

BY
XUAN NGUYEN

Contents

The Ignition of the Dream   1

The Bumpy Start   11

Building a New Industry   19

Why We Build to Last   27

Become a Student of the Business   35

Why Did You Join?   43

The First 30 Days   49

Spouse: The Better Half or The Worse Half?   57

A New Business Model   75

The Meeting Trap   87

Building People   97

103   The Small Builder

119   The Medium Builder

127   The Art of Duplication

133   Keep It Simple

141   Build It Clear

147   Move It Fast

155   Make It Doable

161   We Speak Business

169   Building the Base

179   Building a Big Baseshop

187   The Builder's Mindset

191   Recruiting Mentality

201   Fast Start Mentality

209   Meeting Mentality

221   Teamwork Mentality

233   Selling The Dream or Selling The Business?

Disclaimer

Foreword

Since starting the business 28 years ago, I went through different stages of struggle, survival, learning, confusion, understanding and eventually success in the business. When I started, I thought I was in financial services. Later on, I realized we are in the business of building people. This is our true mission. I must admit I have a lot to learn as this is an ongoing process. Thus, I did not want to write a book about my achievement. Nor did I want to have another motivational book. My purpose is to make a contribution to the people we serve.

I settled with the idea of sharing my personal experiences during the course of doing the business—a journey of a builder. Every day, many young builders embark on the new path. They want to know what lies ahead. Someone once said the best way to know the road is just to ask the person who came back. I walked on that path a few times. I want to show the way. Of course, each person must take their own steps. They must endure and reach the destination on their own.

Like a traveler, I don't plan to describe a perfect road. I'm just sharing my observations, thoughts and feelings during the journey. These are some of the important moments, life-changing events and challenges that impact us throughout our business life. The future builder will recognize similar situations. If they are aware of them, they may be better prepared to overcome these challenges.

In this business, every moment we have, good or bad, high or low, becomes a part of us. For those who want to build, who commit to be in the business of building people, we soon find out we ended up building ourselves. Like a farmer who works the land, nurtures it and protects it, he becomes a part of the land, and the land becomes a part of him.

As we build people, our team is a part of us, and we are a part of the team. This book is dedicated to our teammates, our companions on the journey of finding who we are and where our destination is. As we move forward, we can share our experiences with future generations.

I hope my experiences may connect with current and future builders, paving the way to change their lives by building people.

Your teammate,

Xuan Nguyen

System Builder

Editor's Note

I've listened to my dad talk about the business all my life. Funny thing is, I don't get bored of it. I think it's because when he talks about the business, he's really talking about life. His life. Everybody's life.

That's probably why my dad has always called this business "the people business". In recent years, he told me he wanted to write a book about building people. He had already written *The Moment of Truth* and *The System Builder* books. These books served two important purposes. The former answered the difficult questions people face when doing the business. The latter explains how anybody can build a big business with a duplicatable system.

This book, however, is more personal. While it also answers difficult questions and teaches people how to build the business, it's basically a history of my dad's life and the lives of the team members. It chronicles their personal struggles, their team triumphs, what they thought and how they felt. I hope the experiences of building people shared in this book enrich one another's journeys.

1

THE
IGNITION OF THE
DREAM

*"The best way to make your
dreams come true is to wake up."*

PAUL VALERY

MAGINE GOING ON A CAMPING TRIP, starting a campfire, then letting the fire die down. You pour water over it and go on with your daytime activities. In the evening you come back to camp to start the fire again only to realize under those ashes, there are some burnt embers still red and hot. A strong wind passes by, blowing away those ashes, lighting up the burnt wood. Sparks ignite into flame. A wildfire rages.

When I turned 36 years old, I felt like those buried embers. All my hopes and dreams were disappearing in the busy life of a demanding job, family, traffic, bills and social obligations. I was busy all the time and didn't get much done. I wasn't poor. I just didn't have money. I tried several different jobs. I got involved in a business but backed out quickly. I joined a network marketing opportunity but felt disconnected. Even outside of work, I was getting bored with all the weekend birthdays, bbqs and sporting events.

Many times I thought to myself, "How did I get here?" Maybe I got married too young. Maybe my wife and I had kids too soon. Maybe I should have held on and not bought a house so early. Maybe that's why I can't get another degree or a better job. I felt burned, like dead wood.

I was a low key guy, almost invisible. In the spring of 1985, a man walked into my office and invited me to a BPM, a business presentation meeting. Smelling a network marketing deal, I gave him an empty promise and didn't show up. He came back the next week to invite me again. I got curious and wanted to come, but something held me back at the last minute. I stood him up a second time. After that, he never returned. It was the breeze before the first spark.

> *"Most of us have a big dream. The question is whether we recognize it and are aware of it or we just ignore it and abandon it."*

A few weeks later I bumped into a lady in the hallway of my office. She invited me to the same meeting. This time I was ready and willing.

The BPM meeting that Saturday morning was the strong wind of my life. It blew me away. It fired me up. Up until that point, I was burning inside, but the flames of desire had found no oxygen. The dream that was buried inside finally burst out with the air of hope. I realized my dream was still alive, that it was always there. It just finally woke up.

I think everybody has a dream. When I was a kid, I was fascinated with pictures and stories of faraway places. I always wanted to get out of my neighborhood—the poverty, the war, the old traditions. I wished I was a bird, so I could fly all over the world. Like a miracle, the war ended in 1975. I ran away and found myself in the US. I was so happy to be here. I was free and ready to go. But reality set in—the settlement in a new land, the struggle to survive, the maintenance of a busy life. All around me, in the land of opportunity, everybody got busy their entire life, then died. My situation was almost the same. For 10 years, I didn't go anywhere. Most of my vacations were short road trips to Southern California where I stayed at a friend's or relative's house and went back home. I was stuck in a rut, and my dream slowly disappeared with every passing year.

In the past 28 years, meeting and talking to countless numbers of people, I found a good majority of them lost their dream due to many different reasons or excuses.

◆ *No time.* When we are in our 20s, we are busy finishing school. Finally out of college, we look for a job and want to make a good impression at work. We get married and start a family by our 30s.

A new house and kids take all our time. We are busier into our 40s as job pressure mounts, not to mention more expenses, more debt and more work with the growing children. By our 50s, we work harder to keep our job or have to get retrained to learn new technology. Our kids' college bills pile up. Our parents are getting old and need help. We're exhausted by our 60s and fear retirement without enough savings.

In this day and age, how can anybody have enough time? Everyone around us wants our time—our boss, our family, our friends. Traffic gets worse every year. And now there is all the email, voice mail and texts we have to check, not to mention Facebook, Twitter and whatever other technology lying on the horizon. Each day we have 10 things to do and we're lucky to finish two. We're typical modern people—pressured, hurried, frustrated, a candidate for heart attack.

◆ *No money.* It's hard for us to have money. Our lifestyle increases faster than our paycheck. We intend to buy a Toyota but drive home with a Lexus. Our closets are full of more shirts, shoes and purses than we can store, and fashion labels keep coming out with new versions. We continually update our smartphones, laptops and tablets. Our children also want the same things. Many times their clothes and phones are more expensive than ours.

Everyone else will spend our money too. We're invited to all kinds of parties and events. We're so popular we don't want to disappoint people. All of these unpredictable expenses will blow away our budget. If we lose our job, our finances will collapse. Many people are just one paycheck away from bankruptcy. We have neither the time nor money to do anything. I know. I was one of them.

◆ *No motivation.* Our coworker talks about getting laid off as well as problems with the manager. Our friends talk casually about current events or celebrities. Everyone feels lucky just to have a job. They feel bad for the ones who don't have one. Everyone tells us to take it easy. *Que sera sera.* At home we hardly talk with our spouse about anything other than how to deal with the children and the bills. We like to talk about our problems. And we like to talk about other people's problems.

◆ *Indifference.* We become settled and accept things the way they are. We lose our courage. We analyze everything, the pros and the cons, so we don't have to do anything. We're afraid to make a mistake. We end up talking about things that are safe to talk about. We chat, text, talk and post pictures about the food we ate and the party we attended. When we were young, we complained that our mom picked us up late and talked too much on the phone. We complained that our dad just sits on the couch cheering for some unknown ball players. Now we are doing the same. Life has come full circle. Indifference is the numbness of the soul, the last nail in the coffin of our dream.

WE MUST TAKE CONTROL OF OUR LIVES, WE MUST REIGNITE OUR DREAM

People do such good things for others. We work hard for our boss. We get good grades to make our parents proud. We sacrifice for our family members. We do things for others but fail to do things for ourselves. We live our lives for others but unfortunately forget our own needs. We forget our own purpose, our own happiness and our own dream.

◆ *Believe in miracles.* Albert Einstein said, "There are only two ways to live your life. One is as though nothing is a miracle. The other is as though everything is a miracle." Every Tuesday night and Saturday morning when I walk into the office for the BPM, it feels as if I'm walking past the gate into

Heaven. That first BPM I saw changed my life. It changed thousands of families' lives. Now when I do the BPM, I see miracles in the eyes of the new recruit and the trainee who brought him or her in.

◆ *Have a life of purpose.* Have you ever asked yourself…

If you had one minute to live, what will you say to your spouse and children?

If you had one hour to live, who would you want to spend time with?

If you had one day to live, what is the most important thing you would want to do?

If you had one month to live, how would you like to see things properly prepared for your loved ones?

If you had one year to live, what priorities must you complete?

If you had five years to live, what would you want to do for your family, people you care about and especially you?

One of our MDs in Chicago passed away in April 2012. He joined our business the prior year, knowing he had terminal cancer. He was probably the happiest, most positive person you could ever meet.

Every day he went to work despite his weakened condition and always fought to win, all while battling his illness. He often called his SMD just to thank him for having him in the business. Even through the last days of his life, he had an urgent purpose. He wanted to build a team and leave a legacy for his wife and family. The last week of his life, he kept making presentations, recruiting and selling even while in the hospital. He died a happy man.

We have one life to live, and life is short. Every minute that goes by without a purpose is a minute lost. Some people wait until late in life to make a bucket list. Why don't you make a dream list for yourself today? That's not to say that you put down the big house and the fast car, although that's fine if that's what is important to you. But I want you to reach deep in your heart and find out what you love the most, what you care about the most and what you want to become the most. You will be surprised to find what you have inside you.

> *"How much time do you have left? And what would you do with it?"*

◆ *Believe in your dream.* This is your dream. Take possession of it. It's yours. No one understands it.

No one can take it from you. Thus, don't let the doubters and naysayers destroy your dream.

◆ *Live your dream.* A climber who struggles every step to conquer Mt. Everest is living their dream. An athlete who is training for the Olympics is definitely living their dream. As for me, to be in business and be my own boss is a dream come true. You don't need to wait until you make big money and have an important title to live your dream. You live your dream every day.

I remember when I received my first check, it was too small to compare with the money I make now. But it made me so happy, a lot more than today. I lived my dream every night going out doing presentations, sharing my story and sharing my dream. I felt as if I was the luckiest person in the world. I had a job. I also had a great business. I did have failures and frustration, but I quickly knew that is part of the challenge I needed to overcome to build a bigger dream.

I feel so privileged to have a business that can help peoples' dreams come true. The greatest achievement a person can have is the ability to share their dream. When we live our dream, we become the spark that ignites other people's dreams.

2

THE
BUMPY START

*"The road is not difficult because of rivers or mountains.
It is difficult because of your fear of the rivers and mountains."*

VIETNAMESE PROVERB

THE VERY FIRST DAY AFTER I ATTENDED THE BUSINESS PRESENTATION MEETING, I ran into a big wall of opposition and rejection. The following weeks were even worse. I endured ridicule. People avoided me. The whole world around me became totally different. The people closest to me suddenly seemed so distant. The people I thought trusted me showed great doubt. And the people I thought looked up to me now had a strange look on their face.

I think the most shocking thing that affects a new recruit is this upside down attitude of their friends and family. At first, I thought there was something wrong with my business and with me. Why was there such a drastic reaction from them? What was worse, few of them even took time to listen. Barely anybody told me exactly what was wrong. They just threw out general remarks, questioning the downside of the business.

"Are you sure it's a real business?" … "Is that a multi-level, network marketing, pyramid scheme?" … "A lot of people tried it already. It won't work." … "Don't do it. You will lose a lot of friends." … "You'll waste your time. You will spend a lot of time and make no money." … "They just want to sell to you and drop you." … "Who's going to buy from

you? You will run out of market soon." ... "I'm busy.
I don't have time." ... "Money is not everything.
Family is more important." ... "Only the top people
make money. They are just using the new people."
... "When you make money, come back and see
me." ... And more...

IS THERE SOMETHING WRONG WITH ME?

Like most people, I wanted to be a good person.
In everything I do, I behaved in such a way that
won't hurt or damage my relationships with my
close ones. Not only that, I went out of my way to
make people happy. So when I joined the business,
these reactions from my friends and family at
first shocked me, then puzzled me and finally
depressed me.

I didn't really start yet, and the criticisms already
felt so painful. I felt as if I was climbing a mountain
and falling down fast, getting bruises all over my
body. I asked myself: Is it worth going through
these incredible challenges and end up losing face,
losing friends, alienating people and failing? Is
something wrong with me? Maybe I don't have
what it takes. Maybe I am just dreaming. Maybe
I'm not that trustworthy. Maybe I'm just making a
fool of myself trying to do something that everyone

knows I cannot do. Even my wife doubts my chances. The thought of quitting became a clear option.

But I quickly found out I'm not the only one who gets this reaction. Almost every new recruit received similar treatment and hit the same wall. They were just like me. They are teachers, social workers, nurses, accountants, engineers, housewives and managers. These are normal and good people. After analyzing every single person I dealt with, I couldn't find that I did anything wrong. After all, I just tried to share information. So if there is nothing wrong with me, then maybe it was the business or the company?

IS THERE SOMETHING WRONG WITH THE BUSINESS?

The business is clear cut. I put my time to learn the business. The Trainer puts in her time to train me. They don't charge me a dime. They don't make money until I make money. They don't demand anything from me. There are no quotas, no sales nor recruiting requirements. I can do anything or nothing. They told me they will teach the person who wants to learn. I also can't find anything wrong with the concepts, solutions and products. I love the financial knowledge I'm learning. That's the reason why I joined in the first place. It not only makes people understand financial issues but is also important information for them to build a better financial future.

IS THERE SOMETHING WRONG WITH THEM?

My disappointment turned to resentment and anger. How could they do that to me?! I remember all the good things I've done for these people. My best friend, for years we had a perfect relationship. We grew up together and shared everything we had. My brother-in-law, I eat at his house; he eats at mine. We take care of each others' kids. We are such close family. My cousin and niece, we help them so much whenever they need something. And my wife, she seems so indifferent as if she has nothing to do with the business. The rejections from coworkers, neighbors and acquaintances are even colder and more challenging. On the outside, I tried to keep it cool, but inside I'm so frustrated.

Eventually, as years passed, these people bought from me, joined me and became supportive.
It took me a long time to understand and realize what happened.

◆ *They think I made a mistake.* There are so many bad deals and scams around. This could be one of them.

◆ *They think I'll fail.* Like most people, I'll give up soon. Why should they do business with someone who won't last?

◆ *They might have already failed at a similar business before.* They don't want to repeat a painful experience.

◆ *They fear change.* Change is uncomfortable. Although change is inevitable, most people don't like to change.

A NEW ROAD

I grew up the traditional way. I was a good student, went to a good college and found a good job. I worked hard, got married, started a family and moved to a decent neighborhood. I worked by day, took care of family by night and hung around with friends and relatives during the weekend. The path was so well planned in such good order. Who would want to change it?

I did. I rocked the boat. I disturbed the routine. I walked a different path. Before, if I didn't show up at a party, no one said anything because back then I walked the same path as everyone else. But now when I am busy doing the business and not showing up, people start to question me as if I'm doing something weird.

Motivational speaker Steve Maraboli wrote, "People who lack clarity, courage or determination to follow their own dreams will often find ways to discourage yours. When you change for the better, the people around you will be inspired to change also… but only after doing their best to make you stop. Live your truth and don't ever stop."

In those words, I realized a lot of people don't see themselves winning. They don't see they can do this business. Thus, they don't reject me. They just reflect their inner doubt. When they tell me, "You won't be able to make it!", they are actually saying, "I won't make it myself!" Ever since, I begin to understand. I don't take it personal. It's not about me. It's about their perception of their life. This understanding gives me great peace, and I start having compassion for them.

EMBRACE CHANGE

Change is proactive. Passive people do not like change, but without change, there is no progress.

People like to live in the past, the way things used to be. That is impossible. The world around us always changes, with or without our participation.

Change is wonderful. For the past several years, we continue to make changes. Many people ask why I change things when I am already doing well and achieved a lot of success. Why don't I just keep things the way they are? I don't have a good answer for it, but my heart keeps telling me to make change. I feel changing is living. The flower blooms, the tree grows, the seasons change and the clouds keep moving. Standstill is death. Life is too short to stay stagnant or live in the past. Life is boring if you have no challenges. Life is wasted if you don't try.

> *"What's the world's greatest lie?... It's this: that at a certain point in our lives, we lose control of what's happening to us, and our lives become controlled by fate."*
>
> PAULO COELHO

3

BUILDING A NEW INDUSTRY

"Builders are visionary.
They build their future and control their destiny."

A FTER TWO DECADES OF RELENTLESS EFFORT TO MAKE A BIG CHANGE, in the fall of 2006 we declared our effort to build the New Industry. There were doubts about our intention. We introduced a new flip chart, which was quite different from all the presentations we had in the past. The main purpose was to make a declaration, but something was lost in translation. It had no numbers, no charts, no graphs nor compensation. The reception from a good part of the team was less than enthusiastic. Although many teammates liked the simplicity, the easy flow and the new message, the rest were confused and didn't want to use it. Most people wanted to hang on to the traditional way of showing financial facts and figures, believing that was the only way to attract the interest of new prospects.

At the time, I spent over two decades in the industry. It needed a big change. In fact, it needs a revolution. The industry is not doing their job. Although we live in the information age, people are even more confused and have little knowledge about how money works.

In terms of saving, people don't save enough. Not only that, they are in debt. A good portion of the working classes' income go to pay all sorts of loans from mortgages, credit cards, car loans and student loans. People are approached everyday to get new credit cards or refinance their mortgage. They are asked to spend rather than save. Debt becomes a way of life. Despite enjoying the biggest per capita income in the world, our biggest problem is money. "I owe, I owe and off to work I go!" We go to work to pay bills, and we pay them all our life.

For those who save, they put money in savings accounts that pay too little to offset inflation and taxes. In fact, they're losing their money! For those who invest, they put money into risky investment vehicles. Most people buy stock by the recommendation of friends and coworkers. They also put their pension in the company they work for and trust that it will be there when they retire. It's not always the case.

In terms of life insurance, a large majority of people do not have proper protection or don't have any at all. In most cases, when the breadwinner dies, the family finances will be devastated. Sadly, insurance is affordable for most families. The cost to protect their family is probably much less than what they spend on their daily lattes! The problem stems from a lack of insurance knowledge. Americans can talk effortlessly about cars, the different models, the new features and prices, but very few can identify the different types of life insurance such as term, whole life, universal life, variable or index universal life. They usually pick the right car but often choose the wrong kind of insurance and investments.

The lack of insurance protection along with the shortage of retirement savings are ticking time bombs for most families. That is not considering the looming problem of health care costs and long-term care in old age. Both Social Security and Medicare are threatened by a tidal wave of deficits. The biggest crisis we're facing is not terrorism, global warming or political stalemate. It's the retirement crisis. It's coming soon, and it will plague our generation.

With such momentous challenges, the industry has no answers. In many ways, the financial industry is the problem. Bad investments, risky derivatives practices, short-term profit motives and bigger Wall Street bonuses have put investors in a world of hurt and the country in depression. People lost huge amounts of their retirement and large equity in their home. Debt, bankruptcy and foreclosure continue to mount. The life insurance industry is shrinking, and policy sales are declining. Sadly, most agents nowadays are more focused on the upper market and do not want to spend time with the average working family.

That is why we are here. If the old industry was doing such a good job, we would not be needed.

We are so much different than the current industry. For many years, we're in financial services, but we have little common ground with the current financial industry. They hire full-time licensed agents. We recruit part-time people who have no industry experience. They are agents working for a broker or a manager. We are entrepreneurs, independent contractors who work for ourselves. They usually have quotas. We don't. They focus on sales. We focus on recruits and building. They limit territory and products. We can build anywhere and have access to unlimited products.

> *"You never change things by fighting the existing reality. To change something, build a new model that makes the existing model obsolete."*
>
> RICHARD B FULLER

To say we're different is an understatement. We are a totally new distribution system, a revolutionary business model. We are building the New Industry. Starbucks has nothing in common with the old coffee shop. It's a new business model and a powerful distribution system. It's a new industry in the coffee industry. Some of our teammates are confused about the product versus the practice. The product is the same, but our practices are different. The only common thing we have with the old industry is that we deliver financial services and products. We don't have to act like them. We don't have to compare ourselves to them. They have their way. We have our way.

That's why it's strange to see some of our people who are so confused they want to do what the industry people do. They become so sophisticated they want to go after the high-end market. They dress up and talk like a pro. Sometimes people don't know if they are from Wall Street or Main Street.

You should be proud of who you are. Why should we compare ourselves with the old industry? Why should we even pay attention to what they do? We have the most solid business platform, the most powerful marketing system and the best compensation system in the industry. And we have the best concepts and solutions to help families. We are a grassroots movement of families who stand up, take charge of our financial future and take control of the distribution system that serves families like us.

We can build a new distribution system and revolutionize the financial services industry to solve the consumer's dilemma of lack of understanding, planning and support. The future belongs to us, to a New Industry that brings hope, confidence and a better financial future for families.

4

WHY WE BUILD TO LAST

"Small builders build for themselves.
Great builders build for the next generation."

WE BUILD BECAUSE WE WANT OUR BUSINESS TO LAST FOR A LONG TIME. No one would want to put significant effort into building something that will vanish quickly. Especially when it comes to building something that takes years of effort, time and money, it should be around for a long time.

In the financial industry, few people focus on building. Most perceive it as a silly endeavor. After all, it's a sales job, and selling pays well. That's why the immediate reaction you get from the people you approach are: "I don't know how to sell. I don't know many people. I'm a shy person." And even if you successfully recruit them, a good number of them want to learn about the product, the technical details, the licenses and the commissions. Every time we have training, people prefer to attend classes on products rather than classes on recruiting and building.

Why is that? It's simple. People see money in selling products. They don't see money in building. When they make a sale, the check comes right away. But when they recruit, they don't receive any check. Even when seasoned members go out in the field, if there is a sales appointment and a recruiting appointment, they often pick the former over the latter. If leaders have no appointments, many would rather go home than stop by a team member's home to build relationship, motivate, set goals or spend time to do a prospect list with them. Few want to take them out to drop by, prospect or do surveys for building purposes. That's why we have more sales trainers than builders.

Many people who have been in the business for years are very good on sales but have built little. When they start the business, they did recruit people. Unfortunately, most recruits won't stay or do anything. Recruiting and building generate more pain, whereas sales always bring pleasure right away. Instant satisfaction tends to win over the painful effort of building. But then one day these salespeople will get tired. They will look back on what they have been doing. They realize they didn't have many people. They didn't build anything.

On the other hand, they may be a good recruiter. They bring in people by the dozen. They run a recruiting machine. They are great motivators and dream sellers. They're good on the phone, in contacting, doing presentations and making people excited. But they also haven't built much. They don't grow. They recruit a lot, but their recruits also quit a lot. After many years, they end up with a handful of people who have been with them for a long time, and those people haven't built much of anything either.

KNOW WHY YOU BUILD

It takes great vision, clarity of purpose and a relentless building effort to build something significant. Most of us already have that ability. For example, let's start with a project, like building your own house. If you want to build a house, you would certainly know how and why you build.

> *"Unless you know the reason why, you probably won't find the way. Unless you have a clear purpose, you will run around the maze of life without exit."*

◆ Why are you building it? Is it for a growing family, for your retirement, for a vacation home?

◆ Why this neighborhood, this location, this hillside or seaside?

◆ How many bedrooms, baths, parking spaces, floors?

◆ How long would it take to build the foundation, the frame, the roof, the yard?

◆ How much would it cost? Do you have the budget? Where is the source of money?

◆ And more…

You would consider all of these factors carefully, get advice and make necessary decisions as well as take the proper action to get it done according to your vision, within budget and on schedule. Apparently, we are good with building a house. I wonder if we are that good with building a business and building our future!

So, why do we build this business? I believe these are the major reasons.

◆ *You want to change.* You're not satisfied with your current situation. No one will make any move unless they are unhappy with their life. You probably want to change jobs or career. Quite a few are also tired of their current business.

◆ *You want to win.* You want to be somebody because you know you are somebody. This is the difference between winners and losers. Winners will find the way. You look in the mirror, and you don't like what you see. You know you can make things better. You will make the decision to change.

◆ *You want to make a difference.* You fight for the cause you believe in. You want to provide for your family and the people you care about. This is the source from which our powerful energy comes. We fight harder for the people we love much more than for ourselves.

◆ *You have a dream and a clear vision* of what the future looks like. You see what you want in vivid detail. You become positive and excited.

◆ *You have a game plan,* with definite goals and time frames. You know what you must do, the activities as well as the results.

◆ *You want to build it big.* You have a system. The system gives you and your organization confidence and predictability. You must have a system to duplicate. You learn, you follow, you submit to the system and you run the system. Then the system will run your big business.

◆ *You want to build something that lasts* and to leave a legacy. This is the vision for your mission. This is how you maintain long-term focus and endurance and why you sacrifice.

Whether building a house, a business or a future, every goal requires the same building principles:

1. First, you build it in your mind.

2. Second, you build it on paper.

3. You actually build it.

Great builders build great legacies. They build and make a contribution for the future. That's who you are. You are the builder. You are the future.

5

BECOME A STUDENT OF THE BUSINESS

"Information does not necessarily create knowledge, and knowledge does not necessarily create wisdom."

WE RECRUIT A LOT OF PEOPLE. Most of them want to do the business, but few want to become a student of the business. Let me make it clear: You have to learn the business first before you can do the business. For some reason, people want to do the business their way when they join. They decide when they show up, what they want to know, when they get the license, when they go to the field, and on and on.

It reminds me of an old story about a young man who wants to learn kung fu from a famous master. He went to the temple high up in the mountain where the master lived, went through the challenging qualification process and finally was accepted. He felt great and vowed he would become a good student and one of the best kung fu warriors. But he soon fell into disappointment. Instead of teaching him martial arts, the master gave the young man the task to carry water to fill the cistern for the whole temple. Every day, from early in the morning until late in the evening, he came down to the well at the bottom of the mountain and carried up many tanks of water several rounds a day. He thought the job was temporary and then the master would let him learn. Almost a year passed by. The master didn't say anything. So the student became frustrated. One day he mustered the courage to ask, "Master, I was accepted to learn kung fu, but for a long time now you didn't teach me anything. Instead, the only thing you tell me to do is fetch water! When will you begin to teach me?" The master smiled and said, "I am teaching you!" The young man was puzzled: "I don't see it. I don't understand it." The master replied, "Look at your legs, your arms, your hands and your strength. Every day, you go up and down carrying those water tanks. Your legs are now so strong. Not only that, as you walk up the mountain with all that weight, you are learning balance. You have to focus every step of the way. You learn endurance and patience. When you pull water from the well, look at the strong hands and the powerful arms you developed. Aren't strong legs, arms, hands, balance, discipline and focus the basis of a strong training program? Without this fundamental inner strength, what good is it for me to teach you fighting techniques? If you learn to kick and punch without strength or balance, it is simply useless." The young man woke up, bowed down to the master and happily went back to his task. Later on, the master began teaching him kung fu. The student became one of the best students and the best warrior to ever come down from the mountain.

THE UNTEACHABLE STUDENT

I have met a lot of intelligent, highly educated people in my life. These people tend to think they know a lot. Some think they know it all. Few even look down on people who don't have a degree or who graduate from a lesser known college. Many of these educated people have a learning problem. They are trained to analyze, research and look for problems. And they're quite good at it. They can identify the downsides of any issue quickly. They ask a lot of questions and make sure to know all the facts before they do anything. I must have heard hundreds of times these people telling me, "I need to know everything. I don't want to lose face with people I know. Once I know everything, I will show you how good I'll do!"

On one hand, I do want to teach them everything. On the other hand, most of the things I can teach them are out in the field. Problem is, these people just want me to teach them in the classroom or on a one-on-one basis. Thus, I am faced with a dilemma. If I don't teach them, they would think I have something to hide, and they'll become more doubtful. But if I take the time to sit down and teach them, how long will that take? Furthermore, these technical details won't matter much compared to the real life experience they would learn during field training. A few days out in the field would help them learn a lot more than months of classes. They're like archers who want to learn to shoot but insist on studying in the classroom before going out and practice.

> *"The only thing that interferes with my learning is my education."*
>
> ALBERT EINSTEIN

For most people, the last time they learned something was a long time ago. By the time I joined this business, I was 36 years old and thought I knew it all. After all, I was the only one in my family who went to college. I attended all the classes, passed the tests and earned a bachelor's degree. I held a few top positions in my line of work. I read a lot and stayed well informed about the issues of the day.

And then I joined this business! All of a sudden, my whole world began to collapse. Such a supposedly knowledgeable person like me realized I had trouble explaining what I do or why I do this business. I mumbled, I fumbled, I sweated, and that was just a few pages into the presentation! My hand was shaking, my heart racing, my head spinning. I looked in the mirror and began to see the naked truth. I didn't learn as much as I thought.

I didn't grow and become as successful as I believed. I realized I had been educated but did not educate myself. I was fed books, classes and knowledge at school but failed to learn much on my own.

LEARN HOW TO WIN

We need to learn how to win, how to be successful, how to become somebody. Education cannot be continued solely in the classroom. The acquisition of knowledge should come from experience, trial and error. Knowing it and doing it are two different things. We are so keen to make sure children go to school but are almost indifferent about the learning of adults. We may grow old but not grow up! People need to learn what to do with what they learn and direct it to achieve what they want. The graveyard is full of people who are highly educated but poorly achieved.

LEARN HOW TO LEARN, BECOME A STUDENT AGAIN

When attending our weekly meetings, people want to learn about the products and financial information. A good number of them don't like the motivation, the success stories, the recognition and the sharing by the team members about their mission and their dreams. They call it "rah rah!" Some boldly tell us they don't need the motivation. Just show them how to make money is all they want.

But we are teaching them exactly that—how to make money. Facts and figures won't make money. It's the mission to help people that drives us to go out in the field. It's the motivation to change people's lives that helps us overcome our fear of failure and rejection. It's the dream to deliver to our loved ones that gives us strength and endurance to reach beyond our ability and do whatever is necessary to achieve our goals.

Like a scientist, you learn from different experiments, from your own and from your colleagues'. You must open up to every teammate to learn why and how they make it—through their successes as well as through their failures. You learn from this man how he overcomes rejection. You learn from this woman how she manages her busy schedule.

COMMIT TO BECOME A STUDENT OF THE BUSINESS

We don't want our children to be late at school or skip class, but we fail ourselves big time on this commitment. Sometimes we show up; sometimes we don't. We don't even let the team know if we don't show up. We rarely go out in the field, but we often complain that we don't learn much. The willingness to learn is more important than the learning itself.

BE COACHABLE

Learn to trust and follow. Few champions in the world ever reach the top without good coaching. You must trust the Trainer that she knows the way and follow her direction. You must trust the system that has been working and is proven with indisputable results. You must trust the company, the platform of support, that they know what they are doing.

If you don't have trust in your leader and in the company, I wonder sometimes why you joined in the first place. So please unload these doubts and fears. Please toss away the pride and the ego, and be part of the team. Follow the leader. Follow the system. And start absorbing. Most trainers, leaders and teammates already have enough of their own challenges. Please don't become an added burden to them. Have you ever regretted all the trouble you gave to your teachers and your parents when you were young? We are old enough now not to repeat the same mistake twice.

Be proud to be a good student of the business.

6

WHY DID YOU JOIN?

"It's not so important what the business does.
What matters most is why you join."

VISITED A TEMPLE A FEW YEARS BACK. It was crowded with thousands of worshippers. Inside, people prayed, offering flowers and fruit to their god. They told me this temple is very sacred. Whatever you pray for, you will receive. Poor people bring small gifts; wealthy people bring expensive presents. There is a fair price for their prayers. If people pray for big things, they make sure to bring equally big offerings. Each of them knows exactly what they want: Cure an illness. Pass an exam. Marry the one they love. Have a baby. Get a big deal to go through.

What about you? What is your intention? Why did you join the business? Whatever you want is the main thing. Whatever the business does may not mean much to you. Just as when those prayers come to the temple, if people get what they pray for, they will be happy. If people don't get what they pray for, they won't believe that much.

◆ *People join the business because of easy money.* They thought when they start, everybody will join them. Everyone will buy from them. They get discouraged quickly once they find out the truth is not what they expected.

◆ *People join for the sales and the products.* They expect to learn nothing but products, financial information, selling techniques and how commission pays. They don't believe in meetings and think of it as a waste of their time. They don't want to go out in the field. They'd rather wait until they're licensed and then go out by themselves. They don't like to recruit. They think recruiting is too much work and too little money.

◆ *People join to learn.* They show up to the meeting but won't go out in the field. They think this is a free financial education course.

◆ *People join because they want to recruit.* They recruit a lot of people. Hopefully somebody will stick with it, do the work, and they can make the override. These people also aren't interested in following any system, won't fast start a new recruit and won't learn how to sell.

◆ *People want to feel good.* They love to be recognized and enjoy the attention of being on stage. They work hard, produce the numbers and enjoy the recognition. But they also get easily discouraged when they don't get recognized.

◆ *People want the title.* Most will fight hard enough to earn the title but stop when they achieve their desired position.

◆ *People join because they think it's very flexible.* They do it whenever they like. After all, they're their own boss. They do their own thing. They can do a lot or a little. Problem is, most people end up doing nothing. If the trainer offers help, they often resist and even tell the trainer they don't want to be pushed.

◆ *People join because someone close asked them to.* They joined to please their friend or relative. They didn't want it for themselves. In life, there is little success for people who join a cause for the sake of someone else. They have no personal purpose, no desire, no motivation and no passion for the business. They're there to support, like a spectator watching their favorite team, clapping their hands, cheering for their friends and relatives whenever they have time.

You've got to have a clear purpose. You must know why you join the business. You reap what you sow. If you put the wrong seed in the wrong soil, it may not grow or it won't grow big. Thus, you must know what business we are in, so you can know why you join it.

If you want to be a financial expert, don't expect to have a large team. If you want to build a big distribution system, you must keep it simple and duplicatable. If you want to work for yourself, prepare to work for the rest of your life. If you want to build, you must work with people. You must be teachable and coachable, so others will be teachable and follow you, and then you can build a big team.

> *"When you know the why, the how will follow. When you have the will, you will find the way."*

In the world of the confused, the one who knows the why has the direction. She's the one who will reach her destination.

7

THE
FIRST 30 DAYS

*"Most people won't survive
the first 30 days!"*

T'S A STRANGE FACT IN OUR BUSINESS, something few new recruits would know about or even understand. The wonderful business they just joined may not last more than 30 days for them. I wish that would change, but in all the years I've been in the business, it continues to happen. It's predictable, more predictable than the weather. When we see dark clouds gather, the cold wind blowing, we know rain will follow. Same goes with the new recruit in our business. We need to understand the reasons for this short business lifespan and find ways to fix it.

◆ *The main reason why most people quit* is because they are unprepared for the sudden changes of starting a new business. Most businesses require a lot of capital, know how and commitment to work hard. Most businesspeople devote a significant amount of time to learn and build a business. Thus, a typical entrepreneur would put in much preparation and planning before they start up. That readiness is not often understood by the new recruit in our business.

◆ *Excitement is temporary.* Commitment is permanent. Excitement usually is followed by disappointment. It's a natural reaction. It's great that excitement gives us the courage to overcome our fears and helps us to make the decision to start a new business. But we need commitment to learn, endure and treat it like a true business.

◆ *See yourself as a businessperson.* If you don't see yourself as a businessperson, you won't be in business. Put effort into your new role. Take pride in your business. The lack of confidence and the doubts about your success are big starting hurdles. Although you are allowed to start part-time on a flexible schedule, make no mistake: This is a serious business. A large majority of people in this industry are full time. Many of them put in a considerable investment of time, money and effort. Our system allows us to start with a different approach. We make it easier to start out—part-time, step by step, following the trainer.

When I joined, I made a commitment to treat it like a real business. I told myself I have a "part-time" job from 8am to 5pm and a full-time business from 5pm to 11pm. Similarly, I had a friend who had a job but owned a gas station. Everyday, during the lunch hour, he rushed to his business for a brief visit, and right after work he went directly to his gas station and stayed until late. I did exactly that. At lunch, I grabbed a sandwich and went to the office. I brought apps, paperwork, visited my trainers, asked them questions, observed how they worked and did interviews. And the minute I got out of my job, I went straight to my appointments, did drop bys and made presentations until late. It's my business, and I will make it work. That's my motto.

◆ *Become a trainee.* When you pay $100 to join, you're just a new recruit. You must decide to become a trainee, follow a trainer and engage. Most people fail because they fail to make this decision. They put one foot in, with their other foot still out. In fact, most never give it a shot. Hesitation becomes doubt. Doubt turns into fear. Fear leads to inaction. By then, you're out of the game.

◆ *Get licensed.* Not only must you start the licensing process. You should complete your license in the first 30 days. Every business needs a license. When you get licensed, you are in business. Do you know that a good percentage of people fail to start licensing, and many start the process but never complete it? It's funny how we put in 12 years of general education and another four years in college to get a degree, but most are not willing to put in 30 days to get a license. The degree gives you a job, while the license gives you a business. Between your job mentality and your business mindset, which one is stronger? Lack of seriousness in the licensing process tells a lot about who you are.

I witnessed another strange fact. Many people earned university degrees but failed the licensing exam. A typical degree requires years of study, and exams after exams. Math, science, law, literature— people can pass all the hard stuff. They pass them because they study. The only reason people fail any exam is because they don't study. It's a simple fact that exams simply filter out people who don't prepare for them. Anyone who studies should get the license.

◆ *Believe in what you do.* Develop a passion for the mission. If you want to do something well, you must love what you do. No one can make you love this business. You must put in effort to understand, love and believe in what we deliver to the consumer and the teammates we serve. You must put yourself in the business by going out in the field to see how we help families and change people's lives.

◆ *Build trust.* Either you trust the Trainer and work with him until he fails your trust, or you don't trust him and wait until he proves he can earn your trust. If you wait for the latter, you are probably going to wait for a very long time. Remember: These trainers were already doing the business before you joined. They'll do it with you or without you. It's ironic when people get a job, they start trusting their boss right away. But when they join the business, they are very slow in following the Trainer.

Not only must you develop trust. You should work to help your spouse trust the new business. Bring your spouse to the office, have her attend the meeting or have the Trainer meet with your spouse. They can help you explain the business to her and win her confidence in what you do. Few spouses would let their partner go out in the field every night with some unknown person, working on some unknown business. It's critical that you have your spouse involved or at least he or she understands what you do.

◆ *Fast start.* In order to turn your excitement into commitment and transform your desire into determination, fast start by using the 3-3-30 system. Go out in the field as fast as you can to see what we do. You will observe several presentations, questions, answers and solutions. You will find out how the business works, whether it brings value to people and whether it truly helps families.

You see the Trainer recruit three or more new people, giving these men and women hope and a chance to start a new business. You see the Trainer educate, providing valuable financial concepts and solutions. With the Trainer's help, you make a real difference. You see how families are hurting due to lack of understanding, planning and proper action to build a financial foundation. The 3-3-30 fast start system can transform your early excitement into belief, confidence and commitment toward a great future.

◆ *You can change your life in 30 days.* I am a true believer in the miracle of 30 days. If you're a smoker and you commit to stop smoking for 30 days, you can stop smoking permanently. If you commit to go to the gym for 30 days straight, you can continue to exercise for the rest of your life.

"Give yourself a good start. Get yourself on the right track in the first 30 days."

If you are always late and decide to arrive early at any event for 30 days, you won't be a latecomer ever again. And if you can go out in the field every day in the next 30 days, you will become a businessperson, a good trainer and a good builder in the New Industry.

Most people won't survive the first 30 days, but you can, and you will make it. Thirty days may be a short period in your life. But it is long enough to create a new winning habit and shape the future you always wanted.

8

SPOUSE: THE BETTER HALF OR THE WORSE HALF?

"They say all marriages are made in heaven,
but so are thunder and lightning."

CLINT EASTWOOD

MET MY WIFE HOA IN COLLEGE WHERE WE BECAME FRIENDS. When the Vietnam War ended in 1975, I saw her again in a refugee camp. One year later, we married in Honolulu, Hawaii. Our wedding was very simple. We hosted the reception in the backyard of our rented house. I was very happy to marry her, but in my heart I felt sorry for her. I thought she deserved a better wedding. I told myself one day I would make up for that shortcoming.

We both worked and tried to survive in our new adopted country. At the time both of us made a little over $3 an hour. All my wife wanted was to be a housewife, so I told her someday when I make $7 an hour, I would let her stay home. Eventually, she became an accountant, while I headed a social services agency. Although we both surpassed a $7-per-hour income, we continued to go to work to keep up with growing bills. I slowly began giving up the hope of having her quit work.

Almost 10 years passed by. We had three kids. She worked full time and took care of the household, the children and the bills, busy from sun up to sun down. I felt helpless and useless. Then one day, she took a second job doing bookkeeping in order to afford more things for the kids. She became more tired and frail. I felt as if someone had thrust a dagger into my heart.

Then a miracle happened. I found this business! I can't tell you how excited I was, how much relief I felt at the Saturday morning BPM I attended. At the time, I had two immediate, urgent goals: to pay off our debt and then make enough money to replace her income and have her stay home. I had big plans for her and our children.

With all those dreams, I was quite puzzled with her attitude toward this business. On the very first day, as I ran home to share the business opportunity, she had a casual reaction. I thought she would be happy for me and for us. Although her mouth didn't say it, her eyes were full of doubt. I moved on, telling myself I'll show her I can make it work.

I attended the meeting and saw many couples work together in the business. Everyone advised me to have my spouse involved. So I asked her to come to the meeting. But she didn't want to. She told me I can do anything I want but to leave her alone. She's busy enough.

After many requests, she finally agreed to attend the meeting. I was hopeful. I thought soon she would enjoy the meeting and eventually would fully engage with the business and support me. In the middle of the meeting, she stood up and went to the bathroom. I sat there, waiting and waiting... She did not come back. Panicked, I asked another lady to look for her in the ladies room. She couldn't find her. I kept looking and finally found Hoa in the parking lot, sleeping in the car. I felt bad.

A few months later, at a good friend's birthday party, I waited till the end, making sure everyone had left. I began to talk to my friend about the business. He was a manager at an electronics company. I was hopeful if he joins, he could be my next big player.

My wife stopped me in the middle of the presentation and asked, "Why are you recruiting him?"

"To join me in the business!" I replied.

"What business?" she challenged.

"Business of making money!" I shot back.

"What money?" she countered.

I was furious. She was embarrassing me in front of

my friend. Instead of doing the presentation, Hoa and I started arguing. I never recruited that friend ever since.

In the following months, I began to make money and save. By my seventh month in the business, I earned enough to take Hoa to Paris. She was quite happy. I proved to her I can do it and expected her to become more involved.

I was getting more busy as the business grew. After appointments, I went back to the office, completed the paperwork and sent them out to the company for processing. Many times I got home past midnight and woke up early for work the next day. Hoa started to ask why I was getting home so late. I sarcastically told her if she wanted to know why I'm out that late, she can get in the car and I'll show her what I do and whom I spend time with all night. I took her to the office and showed her the stacks of underwriting apps and recruiting packs. She began to offer help.

Things got increasingly busy. The team grew. I was running like a chicken without a head all day long in order to keep up with a daytime job and a nighttime business. I skipped all the parties and social events. Hoa attended them without me. One day, she told me she had a family reunion marked in my agenda book. This was a very important day, and everyone was flying to San Jose that Saturday evening. She reminded me over and over that I had to be there. I promised her I would make it, that I would be home early that Saturday and at her dad's home before 7pm.

The BPM Saturday morning was great. We had momentum, activity and appointments that afternoon. The last one was at 3pm. I should have been able to finish it and be home by 5pm. Somehow, the appointment ran late. On top of that, the client had more questions than usual. Anyway, I wrapped it up successfully and rushed home. As I walked into the house, it was almost 6pm. My wife and kids were all dressed up, waiting for me. I could see she was not too happy with me coming back at that hour. I told the kids: "Daddy will take a quick shower, get dressed, and we will be at grandpa's before 7pm!" Her dad's house was not too far away. I had enough time, I figured. I was all ready by 6:30pm, and we were about to go. Then all of a sudden, my pager vibrated. I looked at the number. Oh no! It was the teammate I worried about. This was his first sale. Standing at the garage, I told my wife, "Let me make a quick call to answer him and I'll be right out!" I hurried back to the kitchen phone and called him. The client was ready to buy but wanted to ask a few questions. I gave them the answers, but he added on a few more questions. I tried to explain as fast as I could and went back to the garage. But the garage was empty! My family left without me!

All of a sudden, my mind went black, and thunder boomed! To say I was furious is an understatement. What happened? I didn't want to win in business and fail at home. I looked at a lot of other businesspeople. Their business was much tougher than mine. They put more time and money in their business. Was their family life falling apart too? What about my wife? Why was she making such a commotion about coming to her dad's home on time? The party would last the whole night. Being a few minutes late should not be a big deal. She knew how badly I want to win for our family, for her, for the kids and for me. I asked myself: Why is she giving me such a hard time? Is she selfish? Is she the right spouse? Is she the better half, or is she the worse half? Do I want to continue this path with someone who doesn't understand me, is indifferent about our future and a potential destroyer of my dream?

The more I thought about it, the dark side of me grew. I now understood why people divorce or have big problems in their relationships. I wanted to go to a bar to forget about this sad day. However, I stood alone in the garage for awhile. The anger cooled down. Then sadness and fear moved in. I didn't want to continue these heartbroken thoughts. I was afraid they went too far. Maybe she wanted to provoke a war. Maybe this is the beginning of the end, of our relationship, our family, our future.

At this dark hour, the voice of reason started to appear. I looked back on all those years living together. I remembered all the trouble she went through with me, the challenges of family life, the hardships that came with my job, my business and my team, the struggles she faced with her job, the children and the circle of people around her.

I could see why she was angry, resentful and unhappy. For the past few years, while I struggled with starting up, surviving and building the business, she also had tremendous adversities at home. She was swarmed with work, chores and obligations. She took the kids to school, lessons and sporting events. She took care of our parents and the kids when they were sick. She attended parent teacher conferences as well as all those parties and social gatherings. All this she did without me. She'd become known as a woman without a husband.

I began to see why she acted that way that evening. She asked me weeks ahead and reminded me, and yet I still failed her. Maybe she was about to blow up herself. It's not about being a little late tonight. It's about the frustration she endured for all this time!

I knew she did not marry me for what I had. I didn't have much. I didn't have money, a good degree or good income. She shared a life with me full of hard work and financial struggles. She always settled for the lesser side of the deal.

When she left the meeting room and slept in the car, I was mad. But I realized she was dead tired. She tried to support me, but there is only so much the body of a working mother can take.

When she criticized me for not making money while I tried to recruit my friend, I was rude and tried to prove her wrong. But deep down, I knew she made a valid point. How can I recruit one of our best friends to make money when I don't make money? The truth hurt, and I didn't like it. But because of that confrontation, I woke up and focused on getting results. For that reason, I did make some serious part-time income and then great full-time income.

She also helped me with the business. After the first year in the business, I never touched any paperwork. When I had home meetings and parties for the team, she organized them all by herself. She did a lot for me. But this time when she asked me to do something for her, I messed it up.

Over the years, we had several arguments related to the business. There were times when I gave an ultimatum: "You know how much I love this business. This is my life. But if you think continuing to do it will ruin our family and you want me to quit, I'll listen to you." She never answered that question. I knew in my heart she supports me in this business.

I took a deep breath, got in the car and drove to her dad's home. As I entered the house, I put on a happy face, said hello to everybody and acted as if nothing happened.

THE DIVIDED ROAD

Looking back, I get chills thinking about how close I was to making the wrong decision, entertaining the wrong thought and having the wrong feeling about marriage, family and life. I am glad I survived the dark hour, and I'm sad for those who did not. In the last two decades, working with thousands of families, tragedies happened all the time. Some people look so excited one day but so depressed the next. Some had incredible potential then disappeared without warning. Some had great success and a big team but abandoned ship. Some became big but slowed down, their spirit broken, disillusioned about the future. I do not have a statistic—nor does anyone know the exact number—but I'm quite sure the number one reason for all of these things stem from marital problems.

Indeed, more than half of marriages end up in separation and divorce. As the economic pressure cooker heats up, the number is not going to decline. In the richest nation on earth, more people feel unhappy about their marriage and their future. In the age of information and communication, fewer couples can communicate with each other. In the land of opportunity, few families can join hands to be in business. Instead, they wake up everyday and go on their own path.

After the honeymoon period, many couples begin to separate by degree. He goes to his job; she goes to hers. He has his busy day; she has hers. By evening, they meet again, busy with children, housework, obligations and bills. Ten, twenty years pass by. She goes shopping, while he stays home watching TV. They live together but are not together. They stay in the same home but may not share the same purpose. They don't know each other's hopes and dreams. They begin to compare and keep score and are unhappy the other did not do his or her fair share.

Is family an inspiration to win, or a cause for our failure? When we have differences between spouses, who will win and who will lose? When couples have conflict, each one wants to win the argument. They think the other is wrong. When they are frustrated, they tell their best friends and close relatives their side of the story. Their anger grows, hurt feelings deepen, the silence prolongs. And when divorce comes, they don't want to lose. They hire lawyers. The mess piles up. I know quite a few people who didn't gain much after a lengthy battle and high legal fees. Instead, they had a nasty divorce and became even more frustrated. The children can feel the animosity. Nobody wins.

I'm not a marriage counselor, but I came across a few family challenges brought up from teammates.

One time, I asked the frustrated team member, "If you get even with your wife and you win the argument, what good will turn out? Will your wife admit she was wrong and things will be good? Or will it spell more trouble on the horizon?" Can you lose but your family win in the end? If you lose 100 arguments to your spouse, and 10 years from now you succeed, then your family wins. At that moment, do you care that you lost 100 times before, so you can win now? Sometimes when you win, you end up losing, and sometimes when you lose, you end up winning. In fact, the idea of winning or losing in marriage is a screwed up concept. There is no winning, overpowering or controlling the one you love.

In another instance, when one spouse goes out in the field, their partner gets jealous and complains that they're not home enough. The bird is only happy if it can fly. Instead of building a golden cage, why don't we build an open nest? They're free to fly, but they always want to fly back to the warm nest. It's tough to fight a battle to build a business and then come home to fight another battle. But if we have understanding and support from the home, the battle outside is a much easier fight. We can win together. We can win for our family.

A MARRIAGE MADE IN HEAVEN?

With my personal experience and through other teammates' troubles with their family, I always wonder if our families are fit for business.

Somehow, many of us have a belief that business and family don't mix. When a person devotes more time than usual to do something he wants, not only the spouse but many people around question if he really loves his family. There are times people make a half joking, half serious remark, "My husband now loves this business more than he loves me!" Or her friend would tell her, "Watch out if your husband becomes too involved. He'll forget you!" Even the kids perpetuate this belief when saying, "My mom spent too much time with the business. She doesn't care about us!" I was there, on this path, feeling the pain every step of the way.

I've known women who want to be somebody but struggle to juggle the roles of a mother, a wife, an employee and a businesswoman. I've seen tears from them not being able to be home to have a good family dinner with their husband and kids. I've seen a young lady put on "family court" where her parents and siblings told her to quit this "pyramid scheme" because it was ruining her family's reputation. I've seen a very successful teammate who makes big money even on a part-time basis, but his family kept demanding he quit until he finally gave in. As for myself, I faced this issue constantly my entire career.

Is your marriage and your family more important, or is this business more important? I grew up not seeing my father much of my childhood. He was always away working and came home once a month to give my mother money to feed our large family. What was in his mind and in his heart, fighting his lonely battle? What about my mother? Did she think my father was a bad husband, leaving her home with 10 kids?

Every night, when I was out in the field, I wondered what was happening at home. Every time I travel to build long distance, alone in a hotel, I call home and talk to my wife more than when I am not away. When I had a job, this issue never existed. I was home every night, but we didn't talk much. I was also not thinking as much about my kids when I'm near as when I'm far away. When I'm away, I'm closer to my wife and think more about my family. In fact, through this business, I have more quality time with my family. We have dinner, go to the movies and travel together. As my wife got more involved into the business, we became closer than ever. We wake up everyday, build the business and build the family together. We're in the same boat, heading toward the same destination. That's heaven.

WINNING AT HOME

Is getting married, buying a house and raising kids building a family? Or is this just the beginning of building a home and building a family? When was the last time we paid attention to building a family and building a future together? If not, sooner or later, our disconnected purpose will be the crack in the foundation that will bring our house down when the storms of life come.

Is your family the reason for you to win, or are they the reason for you to lose? We have thousands of people becoming so strong because their family is their source of inspiration and support. We also have thousands of others whose family is the source of their problems and failures.

Over time, I learned the business has little to do with the issue at home. The business may just be a mirror of their family. The seed of failures, the problems between spouses, their differences, their mistrust, their lack of understanding all existed before they joined the business. If they have problems at home, they'll have problems in the business. But if they have a

"Your family problems existed before you joined the business!"

wonderful relationship, business will be wonderful. Yes, you can make hell or create heaven in your life and in your business.

Love and understanding must be together. If they are not, it's hell on earth. But if they are, it is heaven for the family. Before you build the business, you must build your family. Before you win in the business, you must win in your family.

9

A NEW
BUSINESS MODEL

*"A well organized system
or a house of chaos?"*

TODAY, NEW CONCEPTS AND BUSINESS MODELS SPRING UP, changing the old ways, challenging traditional thinking and redefining the business and social landscape. Like most progressive businesses, our business model adapts, evolves and grows with market conditions. We develop new innovations and lead in new directions for a better industry.

IS IT INVESTMENT OR IS IT INSURANCE?

We provide both and a lot more. Traditional insurance companies mostly focus on insurance products, and most investment firms still concentrate on investment vehicles. But things have changed. We provide insurance products and deliver investment solutions as well. We have access to all types of products and services from fixed to variable insurance, annuities, mutual funds, asset management and more. While many captive companies offer limited products from their company only, we have hundreds of products from many different providers. In a way, we are like a new financial services superstore.

IS IT NETWORK MARKETING, MULTI-LEVEL OR A PYRAMID SCHEME?

This is definitely not a pyramid scheme because those are illegal. The regulators from 50 states and the federal government as well as provinces in Canada would have shut us down. Also, multi-billion-dollar companies wouldn't let their products be available to us if we were in potential violation of any regulations.

You can say we are multi-level, multi-layer and multi-pay scale. Yes, we are as multi-level as the companies you are working with now, because most companies have many levels. At the bottom is the production worker, then moving up are the supervisor, the manager, the department head, then the VP and on top of the food chain is the CEO. The higher the level, the more money they make, but unfortunately the more difficult it is to get to the top. The same thing is happening in financial companies. The agents are at the bottom, then the unit manager, the district manager, the general manager, the regional boss and the big boss in the ivory tower. One key difference between us and them is we all have an equal opportunity. Here, we can move up and be as big as we want.

As long as we hit the guidelines, we move up. We can be bigger than the person above us. We can surpass and outearn him or her. In my view, the traditional rigid hierarchy is a much more difficult "pyramid" to ascend.

The sad part about the current financial industry is they can only sell. They don't build, or they can't build. Their companies aren't structured that way. Thus, they can only make money on one level. On the other hand, we recruit and build. Our people recruit and build, and so on. We get paid from the people we build and also from the people our people build. In traditional companies, the agent gets paid as an agent, and the manager can only get paid as a manager. Of course, they can't have what we have. They can't make what we make because they can't build what we build. Many people from the old industry now realize that difference and are moving into our New Industry. No one wants to do the same work and get paid less.

People are connecting with more people in more ways than ever before. Social networking is reaching every corner of the globe. The only reason people label us as network marketing is because we can recruit. The old industry does recruit new agents, but they won't let their agents recruit and get paid for it. The whole issue is who will benefit for the work they've done. Their system lets the company recruit and train the new agent. The company then makes money off of the agent's performance. Our system lets us recruit and train the new agent. As a result, we get paid when the agent performs, and then our agent can do the same like us. That is the beauty of our New Industry. We give our people the same chance as those old industry bosses.

There are still a lot of people who are skeptical about many new changes, including networking and network marketing. They tend to have a bad taste from deals that sell vitamins, juices, calling cards and cosmetics. I can see why. Some questions these network marketing opportunities raise are:

Is the price competitive or too expensive compared to currently available products?

Do these products deliver the benefits and results they claim?

Is there money in it? How successful are their people?

Do you have to own the product and continue to buy more to stay in the business?

Do these products have real demand, or do they just come and go?

Millions of people in the US and worldwide have listened to friends and relatives who joined these "business opportunities". They invested a lot of money to buy and sell expensive products, piling up unwanted inventory in their garage, and have often left these "hot deals" with bitterness and embarrassment. I don't have any intention to criticize these businesses. I do know that not all of them are bad and also that no one can guarantee people success when entering any kind of business.

However, we must have common sense. We must understand basic principles when entering a business.

THE TEST OF A TRUE BUSINESS

It's not about whether to network or not to network. It's about the integrity of a real business. Is the business built on sand, or is it built on solid ground? I suggest you put your business to these tests:

◆ *Is there a real market need for what you do?* When you sell something to people you know, they trust you. Sometimes they buy to help you. But the need may not be there. Selling some hyped up product will earn you little but may cost your reputation dearly.

◆ *Is there a good product or solution for people's needs?* If the products, services or solutions are not good, you won't last too long.

◆ *Is there money to be made?* Sometimes, easy money is not easy at all. Many people join various opportunities, but few make any serious money.

◆ *Can you do it?* Is it doable? If you can't do it, it won't matter. Do they provide a system and the support necessary for your success?

When you build a business, you'll be more successful if you believe in what you do and more importantly if you love what you do. You will feel proud and stay in the business until you become successful. You owe it to yourself to know what you have when working with our business.

We have great demand, and the demand continues to grow. This is the insurance and investment industry. Insurance and investment needs are a vital part of every family's future. With our pen, we can change people's lives. We give people proper protection if something happens to the breadwinner. Widows can continue to pay the mortgage and bills to raise their children. With our help, their savings can pay for college and retirement. We teach them how to make money work better for them. In fact, we don't ask them to spend. We ask them to save. We help them understand and plan for the future.

We have great products. The integrity of our business is based on the fact that we are independent and non-captive. We don't have to stick to one company or one product. We don't limit ourselves to what we can do for our clients. We have access to various providers, products and solutions. The advantages give us a leg up on our competition. We can deliver the best for our clients, the people we care about.

Money is found in the money business. The real test of a true business is, can you make money by just selling the products? The answer in our business is a big yes. Many of our agents make big money by delivering products and services without recruiting anybody.

You also don't have to buy anything to work with us. The only time we buy is when we want it. It must be suitable to our needs and affordable for us. That's integrity.

Can you do it? Yes, you can. Our proven system helps thousands of people achieve great success

when they work part time or full time with us.
But it is a business. It requires licensing, studying,
field training, continuing education and constant
building. It's not easy. It's not a walk in the park.
But it's also the reason it is real and long lasting.

BAD OR GOOD? EASY OR DIFFICULT?

Normal people will jump into doing something
they think is easy. Most people will do things
that get quick results. When they encounter our
business, people say negative things. They tell us
this is difficult. They don't have the persistence
to do it. I always feel sad and happy about this
fact, knowing if things are too easy, most people
would have done it already. I wouldn't have much
of a chance.

When people tell me recruiting is hard, licensing
is difficult, people are impatient, unteachable and
uncoachable, it feels good knowing we'll build
bigger and stronger. For weak minds who quit, the
strong ones stay. For those who don't have
the endurance, the tough ones last. They are the
builders, the real businesspeople. They are the ones
who build a New Industry, the pioneers that build
big organizations and a strong foundation for
their future.

BUILD IT BIG

The old industry can call us different labels. They can make negative remarks. They can spend more money to advertise themselves. It's a free country. But the marketplace will determine the final winner. While they have a closed platform, we have an open platform for all types of products and services. While they build on the manager/agent system, we build on an independent entrepreneur system. While they get paid just to sell, we get paid when we sell and when we build. We are very confident in our business model. In fact, the old industry has begun to copy us. This is wonderful. They have a lot to learn.

We are in a multi-trillion dollar industry, backed by a multi-billion dollar platform to build a multi-million dollar business. Even in the short time building this New Industry business model, the results are astounding. We help thousands of people make good money. Many earn six-figure incomes. Some earn seven-figure incomes. But the greatest part is thousands more people make excellent part-time income. They are the new start ups, the entrepreneurs of the future. In the growing inequalities of our economy, we herald the entrepreneurial spirit, the dream to be your own boss, to be in business, to be financially independent.

"You should be very proud of what you do!"

We have a chance to build it big, to bring in as many people as we can and to expand to as many locations as we want. When you do it big, you help people. You show them it can be done. You inspire the new entrepreneur. You bring their dream back. You give hope to their family. Thus, we have a duty to build it big.

10

THE
MEETING TRAP

"The mysterious disease!"

A young lady approached me to ask, "How do you have so many people?"

"No, I don't have a lot," I replied.

"But why? Look at this crowd? This is not the only office you have. You have a lot more of them in other cities and countries."

"You don't understand. Those are the few survivors."

"Of course not! You are very big. You recruit a lot, build a lot and make a lot."

"But that's not the case! I recruited hundreds of thousands of people in my career, but most of them quit too soon. These are what little I have left."

"Why did they quit?"

"Because they don't attend the meeting!"

"But why don't they attend the meeting?"

"I don't know. It's a mysterious disease!"

It's hard for her to understand. It's hard for most people to believe. For almost three decades doing this business, a large number of team members fail to show up to the meeting, even though we have just two meetings a week. Normally one weeknight and Saturday morning, the times are convenient. Each meeting is only about two to three hours. Still, people rarely show up.

PEOPLE DON'T LIKE THE MEETING

One thing I found common among new people is they don't like to go to the meeting. I believe it's an attitude or a habit problem. These are some of my observations.

EMPLOYEE MENTALITY

Back to the conversation with the young lady:

"You need to be at the meeting," I suggested.

"But it takes too much time."

"Yes! It takes time to learn a new business. Just like it takes time to learn a new job at your workplace."

"True, but at my job, they pay me. I don't get paid attending the meeting."

"At your job, your boss pays you. Here, you are your own boss. So who pays you, boss?"

"I'm the boss?!" she looked at me.

I understood her confusion. I was in her shoes before. When I started the business, in the morning

I put on an employee hat to go to work. At night, I put on the entrepreneur hat to do my business. Then the next morning, I put back on the employee hat. But for many people like her, when they wear the employee hat long enough, they don't see themselves being their own boss. They can't make the change, or it's too hard to make the transition.

LACK OF CLARITY

"Try" could be the word that resulted in most failures. Since people put such a small amount into the membership fee, they give it "a try." In other words, they do it when they're available, when it's convenient or when they feel good. No commitment, no obligation, no cost, no problem. In a normal job, if you don't show up, you get fired. In business, you lose money. In school, you receive a bad grade. Not here, not

> *"Do or do not. There is no try."*
>
> MASTER YODA

at all in this strange business. Here, there is no requirement, no penalty and no quotas, so what do we expect? No shows! We even champion this cause. We tell the new prospect: "We are very flexible. You can do it on your own time, at your own pace. You can work as hard as you want or do nothing." Well, they often do nothing. Our strength has become our weakness.

Freedom without responsibility can be chaotic. But for the businessperson who wants to build with responsibility, it is also our greatest strength. We are flexible, so we can keep our job, our career or our business when we start up a new business. We minimize the risk of lost income, so we can gain experience and confidence as well as recruit and build a solid organization until we are ready to go full time.

It's important that you can do as much as you want. But it's also very critical that you can do nothing. There is time for you to take care of more important things like your family, your health, your spiritual life or things you want to do. You don't have to ask permission or worry about any penalty. For some of us, that's priceless. But for undisciplined people, they totally misuse the privilege.

WINNING HABIT

Everyone wants to win, but will they work on a winning habit? Can you win while carrying a losing habit? Nobody wakes up one morning and wins because they joined our business. You must work on it and overcome incredible challenges. You must work on a new habit and abandon the losing habit.

We are talking about a long period of time to change, grow and win. We don't lose overnight either. We lose by degree. For many years, slowly and surely, we hang around the same folks, talk about the same things, work similar jobs and live similar lives, doing the same routine. Like a balloon, we slowly lose air, deflating everyday. We must work harder, put more heat in the air and rise up again.

> *"Winning is a habit. So is losing!"*
>
> VINCE LOMBARDI

THE NEGOTIATED MIND

Every time we have a meeting, my mind raises that question. Everyone in the business asks the same deadly question. Is the meeting tonight important? Is it necessary? Am I missing anything? If it's not that important, should I go? I've just gotten out of work late today. I'm hungry. Should I go to the meeting, or go home and have a good meal? My cousin just came to town. My two team members told me they're busy and won't show up. Should I show up, or go see my cousin? There is a picnic this Saturday morning. Should I go there now, or come later after the meeting?

Should I go to the next big event? They promote it, but it will take the whole weekend, and considering the cost of airfare and hotels, what does it really deliver? Why don't they just record it, so I can watch it later?

"To go or not to go? That is the question!"

Every night, my mind negotiates harder. I have no appointments. Should I just go out, drop by, stop by and prospect? What if no one is home? It's raining outside. Is it worth it to see them in this bad weather? Most people negotiate themselves out of the meeting and out of the business.

A team member who worked at a fitness center told me a story about the negotiated mind. Every time the gym advertises a promotion for new memberships, especially after the holidays when people make resolutions to be slimmer and healthier, a lot of people sign up. They pay a membership fee for the whole year, ready to make a big change. However, more than 90% of them won't show up after one month. This drop out pattern happens every year. It is so predictable the gym knows exactly when to launch the next promotion.

WHY MEETINGS?

Our system is built on meetings and events. Without events and meetings, there will be no system and no business.

We are in the building business. We build people, and we build people's minds. The old industry doesn't have a meeting system like us because they do not build; they only sell. Meetings are for teaching, training and motivating the new recruit. We build their mind, their skills and their leadership.

When I was in military training, I remembered the drill sergeant kept pounding into our heads, "More sweat at the training camp, less blood in the battlefield!" We attract a large number of people into a new business. Most have no experience in the financial industry. They were never in business, never sold anything and never recruited anyone. We want to teach, train and duplicate them for the New Industry. We train them from zero to hero. We educate them to build themselves before they build others. We teach them the necessary know how to go out and help families build a financial foundation. All of it takes time. It takes months to understand the fundamentals, years to become a trainer and several years to build a big organization.

We are in the business of training. Our school teaches entrepreneurship. Our factory builds System Builders. The meeting is our business. Our business is open twice a week, Wednesday night and Saturday morning. These are the days we are open. You can't open one day and skip the other. Your teammates will duplicate you. Everyone will go out of business.

In the building people business, people tend to follow your example, good or bad. New recruits don't see the whole picture yet. They may assume that everything you do are the things they should do. Have you ever driven in a convoy of many cars? You follow the car in front of you. Sometimes, that car makes the wrong turn. You will also get lost with him.

SELL OUT: THE TOTAL COMMITMENT

You don't try to be a mother or a father. You commit to it. You don't try to be in business. Either you are in business, or you are not. You don't try to attend the meeting. You commit to it.

When you commit, you don't think, you don't negotiate, you just do it. You do it and do it until it becomes your habit. Your team will do the same. They also have the same habit, the habit of learning, training and practicing, the habit of winning.

One meeting night, my wife cooked my favorite dish and asked me to stay home. I did not go to the meeting that night. Every week afterwards, she continued to ask if I wanted to stay home for dinner. I smelled trouble. I decided not to stay home on the meeting night. That commitment cleared up my mind and cleared up my wife's mind. From then on, she never asked me to stay home on the meeting night. Totally selling out to the meeting system made it simple for my life. I decided I would never miss a meeting or event. If I missed a meeting, it had to be something very important to my family.

We are flexible but not complacent. We can be part time but not sometimes. We don't have to play the victim due to our poor habits or lack of discipline. We don't have to carry this mysterious disease. We know it. And we can cure it.

Meetings are our business. Meetings are our building system. We will run the meeting system, and the system will run our successful business.

11

BUILDING PEOPLE

"Near ink, you become dark.
Near light, you become bright."

VIETNAMESE PROVERB

CAN WE BUILD PEOPLE? That's a big question. It's been on my mind for most of my business career. When I entered the business, I never recruited anybody nor built anything. I wasn't even sure if I could make it myself, let alone build other people.

I looked at this business in a simple way. I will recruit as many as I can. Hopefully some of them will do it. Most of us see it that way. That's how I started. It's a numbers game after all, isn't it? If they make it, great. If they don't, what can I do? Building my team was a vague possibility.

Most of the people I recruited didn't last. Some stayed, but they didn't do much. Building people was such a pain. Like a young farmer, I just threw a lot of seed on the ground. Hopefully nature will take its course, and a few crops will grow.

After a few years in the business, I began to develop belief in the possibility of building people. The more I looked into it, the more I became fascinated about building, the more confidence I had in the system and the more excited I was about my future.

In fact, human beings built one another for thousands of years. Children in Ancient Greece were raised to be the toughest warriors. They had to pass through rigorous tests and challenges to represent their city. In our modern time, we've developed rigorous tests and training programs to build professionals like doctors, lawyers, engineers and pilots.

We take our kids to play sports to build their physical and mental toughness. We encourage them to join the Boy or Girl Scouts to learn discipline and teamwork. We know these institutions will deliver for our kids. When they grow up, we prepare them to enter a certain college, join the Air Force to become a pilot or apply to a certain program to be a track star. College, the Air Force and sports programs have training systems to help them achieve their goals.

Thus, in our business we also can build builders if we are willing to put in the effort. That realization was a great breakthrough for me because by knowing we can build people, I knew exactly how to win.

WE BUILD PEOPLE WHO WANT TO BUILD

If you want to build, we can show you the way. However, not everyone wants to build. We can't help everybody. There is no chance for us to build the person who does not commit to build. No teacher can teach if the student doesn't want to learn. No coach can coach if the players don't follow.

IT'S A LONG TERM COMMITMENT

You can't build a builder overnight. It may take several years, maybe longer. They have to go through a lot of experience and incredible challenges to build themselves up, to build a small team and then a big organization. My first two years were full of learning from my mistakes, followed by three years of building a small baseshop. By the fifth year, I began to have the understanding and confidence to build a big organization in multiple locations.

WE MUST HAVE A BUILDING SYSTEM

No building effort will materialize unless we have a building system that's duplicatable and predictable. You build a trainer. The Trainer builds another trainer. And so on. If you build a trainer and she can't build another trainer, there is no building. Thus, to build, you duplicate a builder who duplicates another builder.

We are System Builders. We build people with a simple, clear, fast and doable system for the New

Industry. We have a lot of freedom and flexibility to do this business. But I suggest you be in the business of building people. An old Chinese proverb says, "If you want one year of prosperity, grow grain. If you want ten years of prosperity, grow trees. If you want one hundred years of prosperity, grow people."

We have the privilege of building people. This is a big responsibility. People can be built and duplicated, good and bad. In the right place, with the right teaching, they can be built good. But in the wrong place, with the wrong teaching, they can be built bad, and that is dangerous.

I am lucky to be in a wonderful business that built me the way I am today. I was built with a good mission, a strong vision and a powerful system that changed my life and my family's life. That's why we must continue to build it right and build it with pride. Building people is changing people's lives.

12

THE
SMALL BUILDER

"The giant is trapped!"

N THE FASCINATING ADVENTURES OF GULLIVER'S TRAVELS, the giant wakes up one day to find himself tied down by a thousand ropes and surrounded by hundreds of small people. Gulliver is trapped!

I have been witnessing this Gulliver's syndrome throughout my career. Ambitious people come to the business with big plans but end up surrounded by hundreds of small people and immobilized by a thousand small things.

I was there, several times, desperate and struggling. Luckily I survived, but a large number of people did not. They are still trying to find the way out. They are like flies that keep bumping into a window. A few steps away is an open door, yet they keep hitting their head against the same barrier.

Some survive the start up phase. Some become SMD and build a team with a handful of leaders. They make some money, but they see the business stagnate for a long time. Their people are weak, don't work very hard and tend to be disconnected. Unfortunately, they won't grow as big as they want.

These people come to us for advice. They attend trainings, meetings and conventions. We provide solutions and show them the way. We open the door for them, but they just can't make it through.

Why do people become small builders? Why do they stay small? There are thousands of reasons. However, I found most of them suffer the same problems.

PEOPLE PROBLEMS

This could be the biggest one. They have problems with their upline, their downline and their sideline. They have problems with the prospect, the client, the provider and the company. But if you ask them, none of these problems are their fault.

Most have poor relationships with their leaders and don't trust them enough. Ironically, their team also has problems with them. Thus, there is little alignment and bonding to create teamwork. Pay it forward. It's a vicious circle.

Small builders often face problems with sideline business owners in the office. Whether they look up, down or around, small builders are bombarded by problems at every turn.

The big irony is they are surprised about it. They are frustrated and feel they have bad luck being surrounded by problem people. They think it only happens to them. That's why they keep blaming and complaining.

Some of them quit the business because they can't get along with the upline. Some quit because of the pain coming from their team. Some just can't stand other sidelines. They're like a student who drops out of school because he doesn't like the teacher or certain kids in class.

They get so angry some want to retaliate. I talk to them:

"Why are you thinking about quitting?"

"Well, I don't want him to override me."

"But if you quit, you get hurt first."

"I don't care."

"Are you doing this business for you, or are you doing it for him?"

"For me and my family."

"But if you quit, you hurt yourself and your family. You're not necessarily hurting him because he's still in the business!?"

Other times, when I see the upline fight with the downline, I ask why:

"Why do you give him a hard time?"

"Because I don't like the way he does the business."

"But if you give him a hard time, he won't produce. What good is it for you when you don't make money?"

"I don't care!"

"So why do you build this business if you don't care to make money?!"

This doesn't only happen in our business. I've seen many business partners argue their way to failure. Welcome to the people problem business. What do you expect, a problem-free business? In fact, the bigger you are, the bigger the people problems you will face.

Regarding the "upline", "downline" and "sideline", these labels can be frequently misunderstood when differentiating the relationships. For lack of a better word, uplines and downlines are simply people coded above or below you in the same hierarchy. Sidelines, meanwhile, come from an outside hierarchy. In our business, whether upline, downline or sideline, each person is an independent contractor. Thus, an upline isn't necessarily your leader, and a downline isn't necessarily your follower.

Misunderstanding these relationships can cause people problems. Sometimes the people coded above think they have more authority than they actually do. And those coded below sometimes feel they must answer to their superiors, although in many instances these "uplines" have nothing to do with their success.

Reposition yourself. Work with the (upline) leader if she helps you and cares about you. If she doesn't, move on. Of course, her leadership is not a given. You also should not complain if you do not get the response you were looking for. Similarly, when dealing with (downline) teammates, you work with those who want to work with you. Otherwise, let them be. It's their business. They can do as they wish. Don't think their lack of cooperation is your problem when it's not. It's their issue.

If you raise horses, you'll have horse problems. If you deal with computers, you'll have computer problems. If you're in the people business, you'll have a lot of people problems. Don't be surprised. Don't act as if you don't deserve it. In fact, you make money dealing with it.

FAMILY PROBLEMS

Anytime you have two or more people getting together, you'll have problems. It's normal. For example, if you're single and you live alone, you have no problems. But if you get married and have a family, guess what? You'll definitely have family problems.

Small builders get bogged down by family problems. They have a hard time dealing with them. They show their frustration and discuss it publicly. They ask others to help them talk to their spouse. The whole world knows they have spousal problems. I asked some of them if they let their boss and the people at work know about their family problems. "Of course not," they tell me. So then why do they keep their family problems to themselves at their job and yet expose it in our business? Their boss and coworkers don't need or care to know. They are expected to handle their own personal issues. All the boss wants to know is if they can do the job well. The same applies in business.

Many also bring up children as an issue. My wife Hoa talked to a teammate who brought kids to the office during BPMs. She told us her husband is not available. My wife asked her if she ever brings her kids to her job. She said she never did. Hoa told her when we started, we had three young children. We had to figure out a way to have someone babysit, so both of us can show up to the meeting.

At the same time, I see a lot of single parents become successful in our business. They have a full-time job. They take care of the children. They are still able to build a big business with us. These people are truly inspiring. My hat's off to them. When I compare myself to these single parents, I tell myself I shouldn't use my family as an excuse.

DISCIPLINE CHALLENGES

I considered myself a laid back man by the time I entered this business. So I was quite shocked by the number of people I met who were even more laid back than I was.

At my job, I was a hard worker. But at home, I did next to nothing. I was a typical couch potato, watching TV for hours while my wife did most of the chores. I only did something if she asked repeatedly.

So when I joined this business, I had to rebuild my work ethic and develop it more every day. During the last 28 years, my body often told me to slow down and relax, but I had to fight that urge and keep myself in the game.

The small builder has this problem. After the survival period, people slow down by degree. They fight hard in the first few years, achieve some success then lose their fighting spirit.

Very—and I mean very—few people are able to show up at the office at 9am. By the time most people arrive, it's almost noon. They take a long lunch. After that, the day is almost gone. Most barely have enough time to set up an appointment to go out to the field that night. Then they repeat the same process the next day.

They look busy but don't grow. They're behind and have to play catch up. Thus, they have no time to plan for new growth. Small builders tend to skip meetings, come late and hang around the back.

Before, small builders sat in front of the TV. Now, they sit in front of the computer.

They are not aggressive enough. They don't run. They walk. What most small builders do is show up to BPM night, put on a show and think that's good enough. They have a false belief that at the BPM, they will fire people up, get their commitment and then expect them to go out and perform. They cross the line from being a builder and walk into the role of a manager. They lean toward training, motivating and challenging people to hit their goal, but they're not doing it themselves. Some focus only on a handful of producers and rely on sales to keep their business afloat. They do just enough to fulfill their role. But doing just enough is not good enough.

For them, physical discipline is already a problem. But they have an even bigger problem.

EMOTIONAL DISCIPLINE

Small builders are too emotional for the wrong reasons. They get angry too easily and stay so for too long. When they don't do well, they get depressed. The worst part is it shows. Their body moves like a turtle. Their voice is weak, their face lifeless. People see it. Their team recognizes it. It affects everybody. Can you imagine going to war with a depressed commander? You wouldn't have a chance.

Murphy's Law rules in our business. Things will go wrong from all fronts every day. People will stand you up. Appointments will cancel. Policies will get charged back. You'll run into relationship problems.

How you handle these setbacks determine your success. The lack of emotional discipline prevents many builders from becoming big.

You must control your impulse. Discipline is nothing but self control. It means doing the things you don't like to do, so you can win. You must control your attitude and your activity. When your muscle aches, move faster. When you feel bad inside, smile. Discipline can bring you happiness, or a lack of it can bring you sadness. You have that control. You can discipline yourself to be big.

LACK OF VISION

When you start the business, it's an exciting time. Despite early challenges, you have the vision to become SMD. It is clear and simple. You know how to focus and get the job done. All you have to do is get your team to do the same thing: have them hit MD and SMD. Problem is, if your horizon ends at SMD, that's the vision of a small builder. That's why so many people are limited to that level. They limp along and maybe gain a few more legs. The process is slow and painful.

Lack of a bigger vision will result in an absence of focus. You don't know where to go unless you know your destination. Most say they want to be a big builder, but their vision and belief are not there yet. They have no clear plan to achieve their goal. Most don't have a capable leader to provide guidance and mentor them toward success.

DISCONNECTED

Small builders are lonely businesspeople. Many have problems dealing with their upline. Some may have had bad experiences working with others and can't wait to open their own operation. They are not part of something bigger than themselves. Like a lonely shop owner on a little street corner, they are no different than a typical insurance agency. Welcome to the small world of the small builder.

Their teammates unknowingly suffer from this small environment. They don't know any better and become dependent on the small builder. After all, he's the biggest one they see. He's the trainer, the coach, the motivator and the expert on products and other technical issues. He works in the business instead of working on his business. The system becomes irrelevant because few can duplicate him. Like water in a pond, once disconnected from the stream, it will hardly move.

CASH FLOW

A good number of builders stay small because of the cash flow issue, good and bad. The good part of our business is it pays well to market the product. Small builders can make good money by just selling. On the other hand, recruiting and building are long processes, so they usually take a back seat. As a result, small builders would rather focus on baseshop production and bonuses than work with potential builders in their team.

The bad part about cash flow is the lavish lifestyle common in the financial industry. When things go well, everybody gets the big house, the nice clothes and the fancy car. They spend money as if it grows on trees. But when winter comes and they face headwinds, their income drops but their expenses remain high. Most of them end up with money problems. Like a boxer who fights to pay the bills, they usually get knocked out.

STAFF SUPPORT

Like everybody, small builders start small. In the beginning, they do everything, especially paperwork. They want to know all the details of

the business. It's their job, and they should know.
They handle the apps, underwriting, licensing
and compliance. The business grows. They work
harder and stay later because they don't have any
staff support.

Small builders think about hiring staff but are
usually reluctant, fearing new people will mess
things up. So they ask their spouse to help out.
Spousal support can be great, but sometimes that
support can also hold them back. His spouse may
not trust others to take care of the paperwork as
well as she does it. She ends up exhausting herself.
Often, she may have friction with her husband
because she is not an employee. She's his other half.

Most small builders come from an employee
background. They're not accustomed to hiring people
and being the boss. With limited support from staff,
the builder is drowned by all the paperwork and
can't escape this administrative vortex. Their team
will duplicate them and also fall into the same trap.
Instead of being builders, they become clerks.

INABILITY TO SURGE

Every journey has its valleys and mountains. While
it's easy to go downhill, the real business is when

you fight an uphill battle. Small builders can fight one or two uphill battles but then run out of steam. At a certain moment in their career, they run into a mental barrier. Some give up on building. Others accept the situation and settle. Outside, they say they want to grow, but inside there is no fire. They're like guns without ammo. At the end of the day, the builder has to put up a fight. Otherwise, they will just stay where they are.

Throughout my career, I observed small builders and the problems they faced. I was glad I was able to avoid their mistakes.

I've learned to avoid people problems. Most of these problems disappeared by themselves. If there were problems I couldn't avoid, I dealt with them quickly and moved on. I told myself it's a natural part of the business. I learned to lose, because if I wanted to win, they would fight me and I would get dragged into their small battles. I had to lose some unnecessary battles to win more important battles.

> *"It's not good to be trapped by small stuff and small people in a big business."*

I learned to control myself, physically and mentally. If I couldn't control myself, I'd have no control over my destiny. Discipline changed my life.

I worked on my vision. If it wasn't clear, my future would be dark.

I wanted to be part of the team. I wanted to be part of something big and learned to work with people, regardless of how I felt inside.

I became fiscally conservative, saved more but invested aggressively in the business. I wanted to have a big business with the best supporting staff.

And I worked relentlessly when things slowed down. I was confident that compound effort in a compact time period would break me out of slumps. I had to get out of the small trap.

13

THE
MEDIUM BUILDER

"The small big guy."

BIGGER THAN A SMALL BUILDER BUT NOT BIG ENOUGH TO BE A GIANT, the medium builder is a big waste of potential in our business. I call them "the almost people". They qualified for the last race but did not cross the finish line. In sports, these are the players who make it to the major leagues, train hard for the season but cannot perform well at a high level. In life, they are everywhere. Smart, talented and charming, they have the potential to be at the top of their field. But they stop short of delivering up to their true potential. They cannot pass the last hurdles.

In 1992, when we moved to the new company, our team collapsed. The product was not ready, and, worse, we did not have the proper licenses to do the business. It took us almost a year to be ready. By the spring of 1993, we cranked up our baseshop to achieve 100k points in a month. Like an airplane waiting so long on the runway, we finally took off. We blasted to one million points per month by 1995. But the plane lost altitude. Our team dropped back down to 600k points per month soon afterward. I felt we had lost our edge and doubted our ability to achieve one million points in a month again.

I made a decision to fight hard. Within a year, we relentlessly built new legs, worked with the people who want to work and launched several campaigns to build a much bigger team. We climbed back to the summit and within three years achieved 20 million points and 5,000 recruits in one month in July of 1997.

Every time you get to the top of the mountain, you can see the cliff nearby. We flattened out and slowed down again. By 2001, our business dropped so drastically I knew we needed a bigger vision. Thus, the System Flow was born. We wanted to rebuild everything from the ground up and embarked on a journey to build a New Industry. I realized when you build, you can't just do it once and hope it will last forever. Every big wave rises, crests, splashes onshore and flattens into bubbles. Understanding this cycle, you must constantly build new waves in your business.

Like the small builder, medium builders suffer similar problems that hold them back from realizing their true potential.

◆ *A dangerous message.* Ever heard someone say, "Let's work hard in the next few years and build a big team. Then we'll enjoy the fruits of our labor ever after?" What a terrific message! Build a golden goose that will lay eggs made of gold forever. That message motivates people to work hard but also plants a seed to slow down. It sets an internal timer for them to stop. Most of them slow down and stop too early.

◆ *The income trap.* When their income rises to around 10 times what they used to make, many leaders are mentally satisfied. Furthermore, when they receive income even though they don't perform, our powerful compensation has the side effect of complacency. Between a $300,000 to $500,000 income, people stop fighting as hard as they used to. At that level, they probably think their organization will continue to grow by itself.

◆ *The title hunt.* Some will run hard to hit the desired title and then lose steam—until they run for another title. This is one of the strangest occurrences in the business. These players start from trainee to trainer, then MD, SMD, EMD, CEO and EVC. I wonder what's next? Will we need to create another title to get these people motivated to move? You cannot run a business based on titles alone. In fact, there is no title for a true giant. They're bigger than any title given to them. After all, titles are designed for small and medium-size builders.

◆ *Early celebration.* Medium builders enjoy their success too early. They mistake the beginning as the end. They are not big yet, but they think they are rich.

◆ *Family limitation.* He and his spouse may have a business gap. They are not on the same page. When the steady override arrives every month, his wife may not want him to work as hard as in the early years. His vision may grow with the business, but his family's doesn't. He fails to lift his family's vision and passion for the mission to the next level.

◆ *Territorial limitation.* Would you rather have one 100k baseshop or five different locations that deliver 20k points? It's harder to raise your local base from 100k to 200k points than to raise five offices from 20k to 40k points. The big baseshop can be a long-term problem for the medium builder. Many won't risk endangering the local base at the expense of expanding to more locations. Their team duplicates them by not venturing out either.

◆ *Personality driven.* Due to their work ethic, good character, strong will and great skills, the medium builders' personal attributes help them get to this stage of the game. They have the trademarks of good businesspeople. But they have a hard time delegating and duplicating. In our business, they run the system only skin deep.

◆ *Big team challenge.* They have problems handling a big team. The increased amount of problems overwhelms them. They develop a philosophy of self-reliance and expect their team to be on their own once they become SMD. They don't reach out to the third or fourth generation team members, not to bother with the sixth or the seventh.

◆ *No coaching.* They are big enough to coach others but not big enough to coach themselves. Most of these builders lack the big picture and can't see their own challenges. Thus, they make no adjustments. It's hard for an athlete to train their own way to the gold medal.

◆ *Build and rebuild.* Can you build a new team and rebuild your current team? The medium builder fails this test. They are one hit wonders. Many teach their team what they used to do but fail to show what they are doing now.

In order to rebuild your team, you must build a new, revitalized team. If your team does the same, you can explode to giant size. Every now and then, when the situation demands a relentless effort, you must create new waves. You must widen the road, creating new lanes for traffic to flow faster. Go out there and do it. Do it with all your passion and determination to make it happen.

VISION OF A GIANT BUILDER

Can you pour a gallon of water into a 12-ounce bottle? You can't. The size of your vision determines the limitation of your business. You can't do the same thing, think the same way, have the same routine, stay in the same comfort zone and want things to change!

Most people can't get out of their comfort zone, especially when they have some success. When you're successful, can you reconstruct a new challenge?

Success can be the cause of failure, and failure can be the cause of success.

Can you get out of the medium-size success box and get yourself into the trouble of a big, new, uncomfortable box? A giant builder never sits on his laurels. He goes out in the field and forces himself into bigger challenges.

When you enter our business, you have to break out of your employee box and enter the entrepreneur box. You must have the ability to start all over again. You must be fired up about bringing out the giant inside you. By the end of the day, it's all about you. Are you a giant or a medium builder? Are you a tiger or a cat? Only you know. If you are a tiger, act like one and do what tigers are born to do. Cross that finish line.

14

THE ART OF DUPLICATION

"Simple. Clear. Fast. Doable."

MANY TIMES I WISH WE HAD A COOKIE CUTTER MACHINE IN OUR BUSINESS. All our problems would instantly disappear. Everybody would come in, start from A and finish by Z. They would become a builder, achieve SMD, run a solid baseshop and duplicate their people exactly the same. Soon, our team would be huge. Everybody would have a big team, make money and be problem free. Life would be beautiful.

Of course, reality is the opposite. It's not so easy. Most builders face difficulties, frustration and confusion working with their people. They build little or have few legs. The results are much lower than their expectation.

About 10 years ago, it dawned on me why I was so confused: I tried to build people. That was my problem. I tried to raise them up, teach them, shape them, motivate them and even change them. The burden was on my shoulders. I'll help them move from zero to hero, from nobody until they become somebody. I'm a leader. I'm responsible for them. They should follow me. But they seem to be very slow and fall short of my expectations. When people say I run an adult day care program, I have a painful grin.

What a fool I was. I gave myself the title of builder because I thought I built people. But I could hardly build myself. I was far from perfect, yet I wanted to make them perfect. I saw a lot of people like myself, kicking and screaming, making the same mistakes.

Many people assumed we are in the business of changing people. We used to say, "If you cannot change your people, then change your people!" I say, stop trying to change people. Instead, consider them as business owners and entrepreneurs.

People join to learn the system and the business. I just need to show them the way. I'm sure in most franchise schools, the instructor wouldn't bother with people's personal problems. They just show them exactly how the franchise works. They focus on the system and duplication.

I understand we are not a franchise. Most of our people are part-timers and don't put in hundreds of thousands of dollars into the business. Thus, motivation, encouragement and recognition are necessary. But in the end, there should be a clear understanding on our part to focus less on the frustration of building and more on helping people with duplication. Rather, our job should simply be to show the way and work with the people who want to work. Just like in college, you can graduate in four years, or you can take your time.

In a similar discovery, the day I understood I should not sell but rather share lifted a heavy burden off my shoulders. Instead of trying to "make a sale", I began to focus on helping people understand. I shared concepts and solutions, and it's up to the client to make the decision. I became less frustrated. The rest of the industry is still in the selling business. They spend a lot of money teaching how to close the sale. Every time their salespeople don't make enough sales, they feel they need to put on more seminars.

Twenty eight years ago, I started with a company whose leader is one of the most charismatic and powerful speakers in the industry. He inspired and energized crowds. We all wanted to be like him, a crusader who changed peoples' lives. Most of his big leaders were also great speakers. Everyone listened to their tapes and mimicked their speeches. But copying them was hard. For me, it was even more difficult with my struggling English and heavy accent. I gave up becoming the motivator and relied more on my work ethic to survive and build my business.

While we may admire powerful people, duplicating them won't be an easy business. By 2001, we decided to focus on a simple, doable system anyone can follow. The System Flow was introduced, and we published *The System Builder* book. A new horizon awaited. Like an engineer leaving the analog era and entering the digital age, our vision of duplication showed us a whole new way of building our distribution system.

Duplicating cookies and machines is easy to understand. Even the franchise is easy to grasp because it involves physical material, equipment or models to copy. But people are not fixed objects. Thus, the art of duplication is necessary for people. For example, in martial arts, the master cannot mold every martial artist into his exact replica, but by and large he can duplicate the same skills to each student.

To be a System Builder and duplicate System Builders, you must master the art of duplication:

1. Simple

2. Clear

3. Fast

4. Doable

15

KEEP IT
SIMPLE

*"The business is simple,
but people are complicated."*

L ET'S HAVE A SIMPLE TALK. One Sunday morning, a couple got out of church and into the car. On the way home, the wife started conversation:

"Honey, did you see Bob come to church with a new girlfriend. She looks pretty."

"No, dear, I didn't see that."

"Honey, did you recognize Mary dyed her hair red? That color doesn't fit her, right?"

"Oh, I didn't recognize it, dear."

"Also, did you see James drive in with a brand new sports car?"

"I didn't see that either, dear."

His wife got mad. "So what are you doing at church?"

"Oh, I was just too busy listening to the priest, dear."

That was a joke I heard. But it happens all the time in our life and in our business. We can go to the same place and do the same thing, but we will see things in different ways. When we say something, people listen to what we say and interpret from different angles, looking for more meanings than what we really intend. As human beings, being simple is hard to do.

The world is getting much more complicated. If you turn on the TV or log onto the internet, you will get incredible amounts of advice, opinions, dos, don'ts, and most of them conflict with each other.

Our business, like the world around us, is no longer simple. We are bombarded with information. The more information we get, the more products we have, the more we feel we don't have enough. The common thinking is: When I get all the information, I will do it. Problem is, these people don't know when they will get all the information before making a move. So they don't move.

I have seen many people spend all their time creating charts, spreadsheets and presentations. When it's time to present, they fumble through their dossier for the right marketing material and fail to connect with the prospect. The result is no result. When we ask them to give a five-minute talk, they pull out their slides and go through item one, item two, item three and all the way to item ten! They never learn to relate to people or speak from the heart.

A lot of leaders also depend more on email and text to communicate with their teammates. Some don't even pick up their phone. We end up getting tons of email and texts from each other but rarely get on the phone to have a simple talk. I went through a few conflicts. The two sides just went back and forth emailing. All we needed is a three-way call. Problem solved!

Meetings are also getting complicated. At the end of a successful convention, people are ready to act. Unfortunately, many leaders gather their team into the breakout meeting and put on hours of their own version, changing the dynamic of the whole convention. They wear people out. By the time they're done, people lose their spirit and momentum.

On the BPM night, the guests are excited and make appointments for the return interview. But a lot of team members follow their guests to the parking lot and talk to them for hours. They dilute the effectiveness of the BPM presentation, dumping all types of information before the interview. And when the guests don't return, they wonder why?

I'm appalled by the amount of information and webinars assigned to the new people, and yet these people often whine they're not learning enough. All they need is a simple trainer who takes them out to the field. That way, they see how people struggle financially, how they need a person who can communicate at their level, not with a fancy presentation, not with impressive data, but with a clear, simple discussion about their needs and possible solutions for their future.

A lot of people I work with gather more licenses, certifications and professional titles. Their language gets savvy, their thinking more complicated. They gravitate toward sales and away from recruits. They become harder to duplicate. They try to solve their team's problems with more training and motivation. They invite product providers and motivational speakers to the office. Their people get excited with the newest product and impressed by the latest speakers, but they always wait for the next thing and forget the old ones. It's like pouring gas into a leaky tank. They look at other teams and other companies to see what they have that they don't have, to know what they don't know. They forget they are as good as anyone, and what they have is more than enough to help people.

Complicated people won't take simple answers. One day, a teammate asked me, "How do I learn the products?"

"Go to the field with your trainer."

"How do I know which client to approach?"

"Go to the field!"

"But how am I going to talk to them?"

"Go to the field!"

"You're making me confused?!"

"Just go to the field!"

KEEP IT SIMPLE

◆ *Make it easy.* Take it easy. Focus on simplicity. Be proud of our simple system. Leonardo da Vinci said, "Simplicity is the ultimate sophistication." We are not simple minded. We simply mastered complication and made the complicated simple. Simplicity is our strategy to win.

I constantly work at keeping things simple. I want to think simple, make more things simple and talk more simply with our teammates. They should learn to be more simple, trim down their complications and be in the duplication business.

◆ *Keep your presentation simple.* People prefer to see your passion and conviction on the key issues rather than hear lengthy explanations on many different subjects. Excessive talk results in inaction, and inaction brings no result.

◆ *Keep your operation and your training simple.* You'll minimize the friction among moving parts. Your team's confidence will rise, and their activity will increase.

◆ *Keep your life simple.* Enjoy your success, but don't overdo it. There was a period during the 1990's when our people got into fancy cars and expensive homes. Unfortunately, many people tried to duplicate that and ended up getting into financial trouble. It's ironic when we try to help people get out of financial problems, yet we are the ones who fall into them.

Simplicity is essential for your organization. When you have a culture of simplicity, your team will be less distracted, less problematic and more focused on duplicating new builders and expanding their distribution system.

16

BUILD IT CLEAR

*"It doesn't matter what you show.
What matters is whether it's clear
for them to understand."*

WHEN I WAS A KID, OUR GYM COACH TRIED TO TEACH OUR CLASS TO MARCH IN UNISON. It was supposed to be simple. As he counted one, two, one, two, we stepped left foot, right foot, left foot, right foot. It took us hours to get it right. The next week when we marched again, many of us got it wrong. The task was simple, the instruction was clear, but many of the kids couldn't keep up.

Clarity is the other side of the simplicity coin. You got to be simple to be clear and clear to be simple. Keeping it simple is hard. Keeping it clear is tougher. When we travel, a clear sign makes a big difference whether we get to our destination or get lost in frustration.

How many of us went down this road of building and were confused by mixed messages, conflicting instructions and inconsistent actions? A large number of people are more confused after a convention than before it. When you listen to a vague presentation, you have problems understanding the purpose of the talk. One guy tells you to be frugal. The other shows all the toys he owns. One tells you to recruit everybody. The other says to avoid the wrong market. One tells you to take care of your family first. The other tells you to go out and work hard for your family's future. One tells you to run for promotion. The other says to walk to your promotion. You are like Alice in Wonderland, fascinated, perplexed, wandering in la la land.

When we field train people, dangers lie with multiple products. When you take the trainee to see the first prospect, you show product A, and when you see the second prospect, you show product B, then C to the third and D to the fourth. When it's time for them to go out on their own, which product will they show to the client?

When you field train, you talk one way with an engineer and another with a housewife. You present a different version to an accountant and another one to a real estate broker. How soon will the trainee be able to duplicate you? On top of that, when you match them up with other trainers, each may have their own version of the presentation. It happens everyday. People get confused and insecure and, as a result, become inactive. What if every McDonald's restaurant cooked their food in different ways and with different flavors? It probably wouldn't work.

It takes a lot more discipline to make it clear. After every field training, my success does not depend on whether I closed the sale or got a new recruit to join. It depends on the trainee. If he tells me the training today made him more clear about the sale and the concepts, I know it's a big step. When we recruit, he should be more clear about our vision and our system. He should better understand how to help a new person get into the business. For us, that is success.

ONE DREAM, ONE VISION

Many mistake the freedom to build as a freedom of style. They do it any way they want. They get on the road and drive their own route. Soon they will get lost.

I was there, stuck, trapped in chaos and confusion. By 1998, the team was bogged down. And by 2000, we faced devastation. Each of our leaders did their own thing. Each team had their own presentation. It was the end of growth and the disintegration of building. We had so many systems that we had no system. With so many different presentations, we had confusion and separation, not clarity or unity. We were more or less a gathering of different agencies. If you went from one office to the next, you would think you went to different companies.

Unification is clarification. Unity is required to keep the system working. The lack of a unified system hurts so many potential great builders. They become victims of their own creation. I knew we had to have unity or die. It was the survival of the builders. It was the beginning of the System Builder, the people who build a big business with a simplified and unified system.

For the past 10 years, we worked hard to keep it simple and especially clear. We unified together, agreeing on simple flipcharts, training manuals and interviews. We also unified on how to approach, stop by and drop by with the survey card. We constantly train and repeat trainings to keep us all on the same page, to keep the team clear about what to do.

We all do 3-3-30 and are proud to wear the MD Club shirt. We work hard for 5-5-30, and we fight for 10-10-30 to be part of the Great Leadership Generation. We qualify for MD and all wear MD jackets when we attend the meeting. The team grows through simple monitoring when 3, 5, 10 or 30 people show up to the meeting. Then we run for the green jacket.

We know exactly how to win. We have the most simple and clear team in the history of our building career. From the top person to the newly joined, we know exactly the steps to the next level, and this unity builds trust in each other and the whole building system.

17

MOVE IT
FAST

"Life is short for the slow man!"

ONE DAY I WENT TO LUNCH WITH ONE OF OUR LEADERS. The restaurant was not that busy, but the service was very slow. It took awhile for our order to be taken and the food to be served. The waiter seemed to not even pay attention to us. My leader was unhappy and complained constantly. I started to smile. Curious, he asked what was so funny. I didn't know what to say and changed the subject. But I was thinking about his way of doing the business.

I heard several complaints from his teammates about his snail-like action. His team can't get him to do anything right away. He is not very busy. Still, he doesn't respond to his team's requests in a timely manner. He hardly fast starts the new people. He lets them do whatever they want. He doesn't even notice that his people are frustrated when dealing with him. He's like a father who lies on the couch while his kids do all the chores.

We have quite a few people like that in the business. They probably don't understand that our business is no different than other businesses. We do have customers, and the customers need to be taken care of as soon as possible. Our main customers are our teammates who bought into our business and need our support to build their business, especially the newly joined recruit.

Fast is what good business practice is all about. Customers and clients deserve a prompt response whether you serve food, fix cars, sell merchandise or give financial advice. If not, we will lose them. Our business won't last.

In building our business, the freedom of a flexible, part-time schedule can be problematic. Most people start out the business never having been in business before. We have no quotas, deadlines nor requirements, and most go through the start up phase at a slow pace. That becomes their pattern of doing business. It takes them forever to get anything done. The 3-3-30 should be completed in less than 30 days, but most won't do anything until months later. The same applies for the license. It's appalling to see highly educated people fail the simple test, yet many who have challenges with English pass it the first time. The flipchart is as simple as point and read, with only a handful of pages. However, many won't be able to do it until several months later. As for building an organization and getting promoted, stagnant may be a nice word to describe them.

We need to make speed adjustments if we want to succeed. For those who have been lying back, we need to get back on our feet, start walking and learn how to run again.

I was one of those in that sleeping mode. My routine was so set it was like watching a movie in slow motion. I woke up, went to work, ate lunch, went back to work, got home for dinner, watched TV, slept and repeated the same process every day. I didn't do much, see anything or go anywhere. One day I woke up realizing I was 36 years old. Life was short for a slow man like me.

But I began to run and made up for lost time. Over the past 28 years, I have been so happy I had a chance to do so many things, meet thousands of people and travel to so many places. I figured out everyone has 24 hours in a day. It's up to us to use them. Either we do it slow, or we do it fast.

THE ART OF MOVING FASTER

I met my brother-in-law when I moved to Honolulu. He's a nice guy, an artist, a dreamer. We were newly arrived refugees, and Hawaii was very kind to us. Though poor, we were happy. In search of better jobs, he eventually relocated to Houston, while I settled in San Jose. I ended up as a social worker and in 1985 started this business. In Texas, my brother-in-law was working as an architect, struggling to find consistent work due to the nature of the construction business. Even though I became quite successful, it took him a long time to pay attention to what we do.

Finally, he decided to join after so many years. I flew to Houston to help him get started. Things were looking up, the team grew, and I believed they were the real deal. I came back many times to help him recruit and train his people. But after almost six months, he was still not licensed. I was mad and asked why it took him so long. He told me, "Xuan, you shouldn't push me so hard! I'm busy with a job, my family... and as you know I'm an artist. I don't work fast. You got to give me time!" He got on my nerves. "Yes," I said, "I know you are an artist. I know you take your time. That's why I have flown here many times to build our team. But I didn't recruit an artist. I recruited a businessman to do business. The team also doesn't want to join an artist. They want to join a businessman. All of our families cannot wait forever for the artist to get a license. So please get your act together and pass this test!" He got the licenses soon after and today has built a large organization in the Southwest, earning a major six-figure income.

◆ *Fast is our business.* It is the fuel for our system. When you look into the four elements of duplication, moving fast is the most important factor. Without fast start, we won't be able to save our new recruit from all the negativity in their initial days. Without a quick response, the team won't receive proper support to do their business, and the client won't get what they ask for. Without speedy action, building the team will be hard, promotions slow, cash flow poor and momentum lost.

◆ *Running is the secret of success.* Every now and then, when business slows down, when we lose momentum, when failure looms on the horizon, I know I must crank it back up. For an entire month I go out to the field every day. I call this run "30 days relentless". I know deep down everyone can make things happen if we concentrate our effort in a short period of time. Increasing the intensity and quantity of our actions can boost results tremendously.

◆ *You can change your life.* You can make a big difference in your future by putting a sense of urgency into your purpose. The speed of your action speaks louder than your words. It speaks decision: You made up your mind. It speaks determination: You will make it happen. It speaks leadership: You do it first. It speaks care: You want the team to win.

I understand one of the main reasons people want to be in our business is because they can do it at their own tempo. It's critical to know there will be times you need to slow down for important priorities in your life. We have that choice. But if you want to do the business

"Individually, we have options. Collectively, we have obligations."

successfully, if you want to help your teammates win, then you have to move fast. In our business, we are in it together. Our success is impacted by everyone's effort. Our job is to move people fast toward their destination. Just like in cycling where the riders maintain the speed of the group, when we move faster, our team accelerates to keep pace. We can create an environment of speed.

18

MAKE IT
DOABLE

"Make it easy, take it easy!"

ONE OF MY CANADIAN FRIENDS TOLD ME A STORY ABOUT HIS START IN THE BUSINESS. On the way to an appointment, he asked the Trainer how difficult it would be for him to learn the business. The Trainer replied, "This is so easy, even a monkey can do it!" What an answer! It banished all his worries. At that moment, he knew this would be his future.

I know that feeling, the peace of mind of knowing I can do it. By the third day in the business, after watching my trainer do eight simple presentations verbatim, I knew this business was doable. Even though we didn't get a recruit or make a sale, I saw how easy it was to do and was ready to do it myself.

For thousands of fresh-faced greenies like me, given all the complex regulations and products of the financial industry, the big question is not whether we want to do it. It's whether we can.

That's why I am so proud of what we do. We make it easy. We make it so doable. The biggest contribution we bring to the financial industry is our ability to turn a difficult sales job into a business that common people can do and duplicate. Not only that, we offer the opportunity to build a big business.

"I CAN DO IT!"

Those four magic words are my motto to build. In everything I do—training, selling, recruiting, prospecting, contacting, presenting, doing the interview—I always ask myself, "I know I can do this, but can my trainee do it?" If I can do it, but he cannot, then there's no duplication. But if he can do what I do, then that's a success. That's duplication.

It didn't take long for me to realize not only that I have to make it easy but that I have to take it easy as well. I developed a doable philosophy: I will recruit the person who wants to join, sell to the person who wants to buy and build the person who wants to build. I shouldn't bang my head against the wall trying to recruit the person who doesn't want to join. I shouldn't be so frustrated trying to sell to people who don't want to buy. The same with trying to build those who don't want to build. Deep down, I want to close every sale, recruit every prospect and make everyone succeed, but that's unrealistic. I must take it easy. Then our teammate will take it easy. We are in this for the long haul. If our people think it's doable and feel that it's easy, they'll stay.

I'm a builder. I'm neither a salesman nor a recruiter. If I can't duplicate, I don't accomplish anything. I see many leaders forget that important principle. They make a major mistake on duplication; they become sophisticated. They hold high-level trainings. They set high standards that are too difficult to duplicate. They make a lot of decisions they think would be good for the team. But it doesn't matter what they think; it's what their team thinks that counts. When they can show that a new person can do it, then the majority of their people see that they can do it too. But if only a few people can do something, that program won't work.

When I was first promoted to RVP, a position similar to our SMD, I rewarded myself with a nice portfolio. Made of high quality leather, my key leaders loved it and bought it too. The rest of the team wanted to do the same. The department store ran out of their supply and had to back order them. I spotted the problem immediately. Those who didn't have it felt bad, thinking that if they had it, they could close the deal a lot easier. I ended up shelving that expensive portfolio and going back to my old one.

The same thing happened with buying cars. Many of my teammates think they need a luxury car to demonstrate success in order to attract people. I have seen that mentality leading to more financial problems than helping their business. So I kept driving my trusty old Volvo until I hit a seven-figure income. I was able to build it big with a normal car. Again, I don't want to impose my beliefs on people, especially on people who love cars. I'm just pointing out the duplicatable aspect of the business and reminding teammates about the importance of making it doable and taking it easy.

BE THE BEST DUPLICATOR

System Builders build a big business with a predictable and proven system. The system has been proven with social workers, engineers, accountants, doctors, housewives, anyone who wants to do it. They know exactly how to win. All they have to do is follow the system.

Our system works and is getting better every day. The duplication process keeps improving and continues to produce success.

We keep it simpler, cutting down all that is unnecessary, distractive and complicated. It's so simple everyone can see it and understand it right away.

We build it clearer. We are more unified. Thus, everyone will be on the same page, everyone will give the same presentation and everyone will head in the same direction. We are less confused and have the trust in each other to build a big team.

We move faster. Fast start is the center of our focus. We grow and expand the speed of duplication to a new generation of System Builders.

We make it more doable. We are getting close to a system that is much easier to do than ever before.

The new generation of builders are probably the luckiest people in the world. When they join, they fast start 3-3-30 and duplicate others to do the same. That's all they need to do. It's simple, clear, fast and doable. They can duplicate it, and more importantly they can help their people duplicate it.

You don't need to be talented. And it's great that your teammates don't have to be talented. All you have to do is duplicate and have the team duplicate the same way.

You run the system. The system will run your business.

19

WE SPEAK BUSINESS HERE

"Your background will not hold you back!"

SHOPS THROUGHOUT THE COUNTRY announce the languages in which they conduct business: "Se habla español", "Nous parlons français", "Nói tiếng Việt". They post signs in Chinese, Hindi, Korean, Tagalog, Russian and other languages. As entrepreneurs, they will do whatever it takes to grow their client base and expand their market.

If you look at restaurants, some attract all kinds of customers, while others cater to their own ethnic market. Although a large number of Vietnamese arrived to the US almost 40 years ago, most Vietnamese restaurants in my community are still serving just the Vietnamese market. They open in Vietnamese neighborhoods, with a Vietnamese name, display a menu in Vietnamese and play Vietnamese music. Ironically, many of them wish to attract a larger, more diversified market. I doubt they will have the expansion they desire. It's the same situation with many Mexican restaurants in my neighborhood. However, Taco Bell and Chipotle are a different story. They serve everybody because they are designed to do just that.

In our business, our teammates face similar challenges. Many team members started with their specialized market and stayed there. The

Filipino team, the Nigerian team, the Persian team, the Armenian team, et cetera—each segment often sticks to their own communities. Instead of a melting pot or a salad bowl, we have each ingredient separated in their own bowls. People stay segregated not only by their ethnicity but also by their way of doing business. For example, people who focus on sales gather with other salespeople, while people who focus on building collaborate with other builders.

Your background and experience could be obstacles holding you back. This might be a touchy subject few want to discuss, but we must understand this challenge. Otherwise, we won't be able to build it big.

The first time I took my wife to attend the meeting, on the way home she doubted whether I would make it. I was disappointed and asked why. "Nobody there looks like you," she said. "You are the only Asian. Besides, Vietnamese people won't understand or believe in life insurance."

Despite her reservations, I stayed in the business. In the first two years, most people in my team were Asian. It was a normal way to start because people know people like themselves. But I believed in the numbers game. If I had bigger recruiting numbers, I could break out into other markets. With that belief, I prepared to do the business with a universal practice to accommodate more diversity. I made an effort to get out of my comfort zone, sought people from all walks of life and refrained from speaking Vietnamese when doing the business. Today, my team includes all types of backgrounds, ethnicities, faiths and professions. However, we are not yet where we want to be, and many of our teammates seek greater diversity. For those who struggle in expanding their market, they must be aware of these major challenges.

THE LANGUAGE ISSUE

In some offices with high concentrations of a certain ethnicity, the ethnic language is often spoken. The good part is people feel comfortable speaking their own language and can penetrate their market faster. But the drawback is they may push away prospects from different ethnicities. Even if other ethnicities join, they may feel left out and eventually leave. I have experienced that feeling many times while sitting among people of a different ethnicity, wondering what everyone's talking about.

I understand you may want to speak your own language with a potential recruit or client, especially in a home BMP or a special meeting to discuss the business. Normally, you should conduct the business in English. But if, for instance, you have a customer who only speaks Spanish, you speak in their language to serve them. That's our strength and our success in market penetration. We are able to bring in more people from different ethnicities than the rest of the industry, and we continue to open new doors. For that reason, we should be able to accommodate diversity rather than limit it due to our differences. At the same time, we should be mindful to not push people away by speaking in a language they don't understand.

THE CHALLENGE OF THE PAST

Many people are trapped by their past experiences and have difficulty with change. They were raised in a box and can't get out.

For example, analytical people like to study products and technical details. They focus on sales and tend to think others are not as smart or professional. Many new team members are attracted to them for their "know how" and start to analyze until they're paralyzed.

Some leaders set standards that are too high. Maybe they grew fast in the business and think people should be fast like them. This creates self-esteem issues for a large number of teammates. They feel bad, as if they are not good enough.

In the name of building it strong, some team members are held back from moving up to the next level. These leaders create a culture of discipline that may be too tough for people to follow. They eventually will lose these people.

THE RELIGIOUS ISSUE

We bring in people from different faiths. They practice their religion at their churches, temples, mosques and synagogues. They don't need to do that here in our business, nor do they expect us to provide religious lectures. They come to us to do business.

Unfortunately, some leaders are too expressive about their religious beliefs, alienating people of different faiths. This misunderstanding can lead to lack of respect for other people's faiths.

Your culture, traditions, beliefs and experiences could be the best thing you have, or it could be the worst. You should be proud of where you come from, but you should know that others are also proud of their identity too. Any semblance or perception of prejudice can dampen the growth of your organization.

Children don't have these issues. It becomes a problem when we grow up. When I was young, infighting between religious factions stirred an uneasiness among our friends. Then we began to hear prejudice between the Northern and Southern people. Next, we learned about conflict between the rich and the poor, between the educated and the uneducated. What a big mess. Our backgrounds became walls preventing us from reaching out to people or letting others come to us.

Descriptions of people are relative in word and deceptive in mind. A rich man in a poor village could be a poor guy in a big city. An educated person can be ignorant about something as simple as fishing. An American is in the majority in New York but in the minority in Toronto. Some of your teammates who have small titles are bigger than you in other areas of life. When you're high, keep it low, and when you're low, know you're someone special. When you are a majority, think like a minority.

LET'S SPEAK BUSINESS

When you are in business, break down these walls. Maintain balance in your thinking and a high level of tolerance when dealing with people. Every one of us is part of a team. We are all entrepreneurs and System Builders. All for one, and one for all.

Minimize the differences in our backgrounds, while maximizing the common ground. When working with other people, especially in the same office, don't segregate. Try to mix in, join forces and collaborate. Eventually your organization will be diversified but also unified.

We are privileged to serve people. It's an honor to help people win. Our diversity should be an advantage and allow us to be big. We can penetrate a larger market, helping more families. We should refrain from polarized points of view and minimize controversial practices. We should maintain an open business that's inclusive, not exclusive. We should respect people for who they are and make them feel good doing business with us.

We unify through diversification. Let's speak unity and harmony. Let's speak a language of a big company and a giant team. Let's speak business, our common language.

20

BUILDING
THE BASE

"The MD Factory."

COMMON WISDOM SAYS A 100K BASE IS THE SYMBOL OF A BIG BASESHOP. But it might not be true as we've seen some builders achieve those numbers but end up short of building a significant team. The leaders bulletin can also be confusing. Some bases have big production but few recruits or lots of recruits but poor production.

Like farmers who work hard on their land but end up getting a poor crop, it could be the wrong seed or inefficient techniques. Problem is, they don't know what they don't know. The same is true with small baseshops that remain small forever.

The baseshop is a critical part of our building system. But what is a baseshop and why do we need to build it? Can we build without a baseshop?

The base is the ultimate building unit of our system. It comprises all your teammates who have yet to achieve SMD. The superbase is your baseshop plus your direct first generation SMD baseshop builders. A superteam is all the baseshops in your organization, regardless of generation. We call it your hierarchy or your team. There are also many hierarchies within your hierarchy or many teams within your team. It's similar to a family tree.

Our ancestors start a family and have children, and the children grow up and start their own families, and so on. While each nuclear family is their own baseshop, so to speak, the extended family is in the same hierarchy.

Either you run the baseshop, or you belong to a baseshop and are learning to build a baseshop of your own. There are many reasons to build the base, but the most important one is to duplicate new baseshop builders. I call the baseshop the MD Factory.

The purpose is to build SMDs who build more SMDs, your first generation front line. However, since a SMD is simply a MD who builds one MD under him, we figured out the most clear, simple and easy way is to focus on the MD. If everyone just targets MD, then all you have to do is work your way to become MD, help one of your teammates become MD, and you will become SMD. This simple focus is one of the greatest breakthroughs in our building career. It makes building a baseshop more doable and duplicatable. When everyone in your team just focuses on becoming MD and producing MDs, they now become a baseshop builder.

BUILDING YOUR BASE

◆ *Picture what you want to build.* If you want to build a big base, you will need a lot of people. Knowing this, you should commit to recruit. You look for at least 5 to 7 front line people. They don't have to be the best. They just have to be committed and be students of the business. The best indicator is their commitment to the BMP and the BPM. They go out to the field, and they come to the meeting. It may take time to find these legs. Some of them grow fast, others slower. Eventually the baseshop will form.

◆ *You must prepare yourself to become a baseshop builder.* Fast start is your key activity. All we do is fast start the new recruit, get them to achieve 3-3-30 and then work with the 3 new recruits, fast start them and do it over and over again. Not everyone will cooperate, but your job is to fast start the ones who want to be fast started. Be the best fast start trainer, and you will be the best baseshop builder. It's that simple.

Fast start is the number one skill of a great baseshop builder. Not recruiting, not selling, not motivating, not technical training. The most important skill of a great baseshop builder is the ability to duplicate. You duplicate new fast start trainers. These people will become your future baseshop builders.

◆ *Don't wait until you become MD or SMD to build the base.* You build your base now. The common mistake of small builders is focusing on the title and contract of MD and SMD. You'll get the contract but will have a small base, especially after replacement. You should build it big and strong now, recruit and build more legs and have a strong baseshop mentality. When it's time to get promoted to SMD and run your own base, you start with confidence.

RUNNING YOUR BASE

How do you build a MD Factory? What does it take to have a good baseshop? You must know what you have.

◆ *Who has a meeting mentality?* How many of your people show up to the BPM twice a week and all other events? A good baseshop increases attendance consistently.

◆ *How many people are getting fast started?* You may have a recruiting explosion, but if few hit

3-3-30, then you have a problem. Looking at the number of new MD Club members, is your fast start program being successfully implemented?

◆ *How many people get licensed and get the first check?* I always look for new recruits getting licensed and going out to make their first check. This would dramatically change the new recruit's attitude from "I'm not sure I can do it" to "I'm actually doing it".

◆ *The best number you want to see* is how many of your trainers hit 5-5-30 and who is the new trainer that hits 5-5-30.

◆ *To keep the MD Factory running,* you must do 5-5-30. Actually you should do 10-10-30 or more. The more you lead in the fast start area, the more likely your trainer duplicates you. It's amazing to see a good number of leaders don't even hit 5-5-30. Most take care of the BPM, training, motivation and compliance, but they fall short on duplication and taking people out to fast start. Some of them don't sell. They let others do the sales training. Some sell but don't recruit and don't take people out to recruit.

It reminds me of a couple who came to me for advice. The husband told me he only likes to recruit, train and motivate. He lets his wife do all the sales. I told them it may work, but it won't be the best way. I asked him, "What if others in your team don't have a wife who is good at sales, what will they do?" I told him not to create an unnecessary challenge: "Why don't you go out to do the fast start and duplication? Your wife can be a good source for back up, matching up and field training other new recruits. You can be the fast start trainer. And if she wants, your wife can also recruit, sell, train and motivate. Plus, you foster a can-do mentality in your base."

◆ *Make money.* If you do 10-10-30, you'll have good cash flow. If your trainer does 5-5-30, they will make money and build at the same time. Monitor cash flow. Making sure your trainer makes money is important to produce future builders. After all, if they are not making money, they won't go full time. It's hard to build a good baseshop builder when he's still part time.

◆ *Monitor and review your trainer's organization chart.* Remind them regularly to build their base. Do it monthly to see their progress and to have a good idea on their situation. You inspect what you expect. People will rise to your expectation.

◆ *Create a culture of building.* If not, it may divert into selling or other types of distractions. Everything you do—recruiting, selling, contests, events—should be for building purposes. Actually, you don't build. You create a building environment and a building culture, and then building will occur.

◆ *You need to train on products, solutions and technical aspects of the business.* Your teammates and trainers must be good at what they do. Knowledge builds confidence. A knowledgable trainer can keep it simple and clear. A poor trainer will make it complicated and confusing. A team with strong fundamentals is always good in fieldwork and increases fast start.

◆ *Maintain a professional office and strong staff support.* After all, this is a serious business that handles people's money, their children's college fund and their retirement. Ask yourself, if you were in the client's shoes, would you put money in a businessperson like yourself? How can a client do business with a person who doesn't have an office and staff support? Your teammate can see that too. They can tell whether you are a real entrepreneur or an unreliable salesperson who may not last for the long term.

All my life, I have been a true believer in a respectable office and a solid operation. No one should ever doubt my commitment to build a quality business. I believe every dollar I invest in my office, staff, equipment, awards and trips will result in a much greater return than what I put in. Your people will also duplicate you. That is why we have more offices and more expansion and duplicate a lot faster than the rest of the industry.

◆ *Don't abuse the meetings.* We have regular BPMs twice a week. After the BPM, there's the baseshop meeting. You meet new people, share good news, recognize achievements, set goals and challenge one another. Keep it short and sweet. Don't keep them with you too late. Most are part-timers. They have families waiting and jobs the next morning. Let them go as soon as you can. For the committed trainer and the full timer, they may stay to monitor, plan and match up, but respect their time. Don't test people's endurance. Don't test their commitment by keeping them late. There is nothing worse than a spouse and children waiting at home, wondering what their spouse or their parents are doing at this late hour. That is not building. That is unnecessarily creating a bad feeling with the teammate and their family about the business.

◆ *Build relationship.* Everyone in the base is your direct recruit. You should get to know them and their family. Meet them and create social events, so they see the pleasant side of our meetings. Not all of our meetings have to be about business. Sometimes, the non-business meeting can be the best business meeting you ever had.

21

BUILDING
A BIG BASESHOP

*"If you want to cross the ocean,
you need a big ship."*

YOU SHOULD BUILD A GOOD BASE BEFORE YOU BUILD A BIG BASE. Without strong fundamentals and a solid foundation, even if your baseshop surges to big numbers, it might not sustain. Although a big portion of the compensation comes from the base, don't build a big baseshop for the cash or, worse, for the baseshop pool. You may get the cash, but you are not building new builders or long-term security. You are not duplicatable.

> *"The archer can't aim and think about the winning prize at the same time."*

Don't hold people back, tell them they are not ready or persuade them to stay in the base. Don't keep the baby in the womb longer than their due date. A healthy big baseshop is the one that keeps producing new MDs and SMDs. Keep more people coming in and more going out. Like a good school, you want more students entering and more graduating. Building a big baseshop for the wrong reasons will hinder growth and cost you more in the long run.

Thus, a big baseshop builder knows her main purpose is to build new successful baseshop builders.

◆ *Aim for 30-30-100.* Build a big ship to cross the ocean. You don't come here to anchor on the shore or sail in a little lake. Build it as big as your heart desires.

If you can get 30 people to show up to the meeting twice a week, you have enough committed people for a big base. With 30 people at the meeting, you may get at least 30 recruits for the base and have a good chance to hit 100k production. That is a solid foundation. You achieve the 100k base through 30 committed people and 30 new recruits, and not because of your sales skills.

◆ *Build at least 10 fast start trainers.* These are trainers who can hit 5-5-30 and 10-10-30 regularly. They are the backbone of a big base, the duplicators in line to be the next big baseshop builders.

◆ *Build wide.* Continue to recruit new people and build new legs. Big baseshop builders build seven to ten trainer legs. These legs will be the source of new recruits, production and duplication for the big base.

◆ *Depth is the root of great bases.* Help every leg go as deep as you can. The deeper the leg, the more leaders and builders that will sprout out. Depth is also the key factor for a strong replacement and for continuing to build new builders. Great builders overlap leadership, reach down and make sure the person at the bottom is being taken care of.

◆ *Teach it simple, train it simple and build it simple.* Look at Macy's. They have all kinds of promotions, campaigns and holiday specials, but they all boil down to one simple thing: get more people in the store. If you want to build and maintain a big base, you have to keep it simple.

◆ *Work on the habits of a winner.* Build a builder's mindset. A smart baseshop builder knows she must focus first on a meeting mentality. Next is a teamwork mentality in her base, then a recruiting mentality and fast start mentality are possible.

TAKING REPLACEMENT

Replacement is at the center of our system, the key to building and maintaining the MD Factory. Having a culture of building and taking a strong replacement is vital for the base and the system as well as for the new SMD who gives up the leg. The person who gives a strong replacement will get a strong replacement. A person who has problems giving replacement will have greater problems in the future when it's their time to take replacement legs.

However, we should be sensitive when the potential replacement leg has close family relationships or any special situations with the newly promoted SMD. We should maintain the integrity of the system while considering fairness among the promoting SMD, the newly promoted SMD and the replacement leg person. Work it out. After all, it should be a happy event. When you promote a new SMD, she will be your first generation builder for years to come. You also receive a good replacement leg.

For the newly promoted SMD, you made it to the highest contract in our business. You've just given the replacement, and from now on you can build a new base and receive unlimited replacement legs in the future.

Without a strong replacement, you won't be able to maintain a big baseshop. You must set a firm standard for replacement that your team will follow. Otherwise, in the long run you will hurt all the baseshop builders in your hierarchy.

BUILDING MULTIPLE BASES

A lot of baseshops limit themselves to their local area. Anytime they travel more than half an hour, they think it's far. The unwillingness to expand limits the potential of everybody in the base, killing the chance to build it big. They stick to a small circle of prospects when they have a much larger pool of potential builders just one or two hours away.

It would be ideal to just stay local to build the base. However, in reality, you may struggle to find enough strong builders in your area. There are many potential builders at farther distances. You don't want to miss any opportunities.

When fishing, you don't fish where you happen to be. You go where the fish are. For instance, if I live in Los Angeles, I would venture out to Orange County or San Diego to build. Anybody within 100 to 200 miles should be in my area of activity. Builders go where they can find builders. The act of a leader going from LA to San Diego to build would expand the vision of their team. The people in San Diego would now want to build LA, Orange County and other areas, and vice versa. The ping pong recruiting will create the popcorn effect in the base. It's like opening a waterway from the reservoir into the pond.

Building multiple bases opens the door for future long distance expansion throughout the country. If you have multiple baseshops, your trainer will travel and gain experience. She will be more efficient and results-oriented. No one wants to travel and come back empty handed. When the fisherman gets out of the pond and into the lake, it doesn't take long for him to venture out into the ocean. Building in multiple locations will lead to a big base and a big hierarchy in the days ahead.

BE IN THE BASE – BE A BASESHOP BUILDER

When I started my career in 1978 as a resettlement worker for newly arrived immigrants to America, I had a chance to meet the head of the organization. In his late sixties, he had been doing this work for more than 30 years. He ran an international operation, providing relief to refugees around the world. And yet he did the same day-to-day work I did. Although he kept a smaller caseload, he would personally meet the newly arrived refugee families and take care of their needs from finding schools for the kids, apartments for the family, jobs for the parents and hospitals for the sick. Despite his age, he was still out in the field! He knew what he was doing, what was going on and what he was talking about.

Be in the base. Be where the action is. If you want to build and expand your organization, you must be in the baseshop business. You see new people everyday. You fast start them. You know their family. You know the heartbeat of your base. You connect and relate to new team members. You can feel the pain of defeat. You can share in the victory. You are in the game. When you train, present or talk, you know how they feel. You know their challenges. And you can offer guidance and solutions. You don't forget where you're coming from because you're there with the team. Your feet are on the ground. You're a team player, a team builder, a baseshop builder. After all, that's what you are coming here for, to make a difference.

22

THE BUILDER'S MINDSET

"Leaders are made, not born.
So are builders."

THE LONGER I AM IN THE BUSINESS, THE MORE I WANT TO BE A SYSTEM BUILDER. I want to build a big business with a predictable, duplicatable system. While I believe our system is proven and produces results, I think we still have a long way to go.

At every meeting or big event, people always ask: "How do I build?" "How can I build it big?" or "What am I supposed to do to build a baseshop?"

We have a simple system for them to follow. The System Flow, the MD Factory and the 3-3-30 formula to fast start are the solutions for building a big organization. We have *The System Builder* book, the Trainer's Manual and the flipcharts to teach, train and duplicate. However, people must have the builder's mindset to understand the system and make it work.

Consider the mindset of leaders like school principals, Army generals or NFL quarterbacks. Besides their know how, what type of mental discipline do they need to fulfill their mission? How have they prepared themselves to consistently deliver at a high level?

In our system, the builder's mindset is composed of four key elements.

1. Recruiting Mentality

2. Fast Start Mentality

3. Meeting Mentality

4. Teamwork Mentality

WHAT IS A MENTALITY?

My simple definition is a mental habit.

People are creatures of habit. We have physical habits like sleeping on our side or eating too fast. We have mental habits like procrastination or bragging. Whether mental or physical, habits are a part of us, and they become very hard to break. For instance, most people have a certain kind of food they won't touch. Late people never show up on time. Worry warts always worry.

When people go to work, they get into their car, take the same route and make the same turns without any thought. They arrive at their workplace the same way every day. The repetition shapes how their brain operates. If they do something long enough, they will acquire a new habit.

Therein lies the secret of success or failure. I believe the reason why a person wins or loses is a result of

> *"Tough people are good at facing challenges, and we can create tough challenges to build tough people. The Army knows that."*

their winning or losing habits. A negative, procrastinating, undisciplined person will most likely lose, whereas a positive, proactive, tough-minded person will have a good chance to succeed. In our business, we don't really build people. What we do is teach and practice new habits. And those habits build a new mentality and a builder's mindset.

23

RECRUITING MENTALITY

"The habit of the giant."

HOW CAN WE BUILD A RECRUITING HABIT? Can we take a new person with zero recruiting experience and instill in him a recruiting mentality?

Telling a new team member to recruit is like asking a kid who never swims to jump into the pool. In the early days of my career, I heard about recruiting all the time. At meetings, there were training, recognition and contests about recruiting. It familiarized me with the concept, but it was far from enough. Like learning a new language, you will never speak it until you actually practice and do it. Thus, the key to our system is not in the explanation or the classroom training. It's being out in the field and gaining real world experience.

Helping a person do a prospect list, going out to prospect, dropping by, stopping by with them, making contact, doing the presentation, following up, doing the return interview—these are all recruiting practices. The time the trainer sits in the car with the trainee, the question and answer sessions with the prospect, the excitement of these activities—these habits form a new recruiting mentality.

In the early days, I went to Southern California to support one of my new SMDs who decided to move to the Los Angeles area. He didn't know many people, but having struggled in San Jose, he had nothing to lose. For almost a year, nothing much happened.

Back in San Jose, we had a good habit of doing the prospect list with new team members and keeping a copy for the trainer, so we could communicate about a potential prospect. We also asked them to list names of people they knew outside of Northern California. Although many people did not last in the business, we still had their prospect list. My SMD brought with him stacks of these prospect lists when he moved to LA. One of the names on that list, a travel agent, agreed to see us. We met, he joined, we fast started him, and our explosion began. From this one contact, we gained a foothold in Southern California and eventually built several SMDs, CEOs and offices.

The habit of prospecting and maintaining a prospect list paid off for many of our builders. When we recruit a new team member, it is critical to develop the prospect list, which is our market. It is also a good habit to get the names of people they know from other cities and states. Overlooking these habits could cost you a fortune. Since a typical person should have about 200 to 300 names, somewhere on this list are the people you're looking for.

YOU'RE ONE RECRUIT AWAY FROM AN EXPLOSION!

This belief is the key ingredient of your recruiting mentality. You will regard every prospect list as a fortune list and every name as a potential builder. You will realize this list will bring you this one recruit, who will bring the next one, who will lead you to another one, and eventually you'll get the big one.

In my second year in the business, Hoa had a friend interested in owning the product. We came to her friend's home. But instead of looking for the sale, I tried to recruit the couple. While I talked about how we help people with our financial concepts and solutions, my focus was more about the good things we offer to the consumer and how our business fulfills a great market need. The couple showed interest and were willing to come to our office for the BPM. I did not make the sale that night. On the way home, my wife was unhappy, thinking I failed to make the sale. I explained the sale is obviously done. They believed in it enough to look into our business. Why hurry? I told her. I wanted to recruit them first. If they end up not joining, I could always make the sale later. Hoa began to understand that I had a stronger recruiting mentality than a sales mentality.

Don't get me wrong. I made sales. However, I always have my recruiting antenna up every time I sit down with a potential client. I always send out recruiting messages. If the prospect shows no sign of interest, I will make the sale. On the other hand, even after making the sale, I would often come back later and try to recruit them.

THE MAGIC OF PROSPECTING

By the spring of 1987, I felt I needed to make a move. Even though I made good money, most of it was due to my personal effort. Few of my people became trainers.

Then one day while having lunch, I bumped into a coworker from a different department. She was sitting with another man. I tried to recruit her once before, but she wasn't interested. Nonetheless, my recruiting habit made me come to her table. She introduced the man as her husband, an engineering manager. My recruiting antenna sprang up, and I started to make conversation.

We traded business cards. At the time, I was still doing job development for newly arrived refugees and told him I would appreciate it if he could inform me of any job openings. I later made a few phone calls to the couple and established a relationship. Then one night, after finishing an appointment, I called and asked if it was alright to drop by the house since I was in the area. The husband agreed. It was almost 10pm. I was very excited. I recruited him that night. The following days I took him out in the field. However, not much happened.

One week passed. At a wedding, I met a couple and started to prospect them. We traded phone numbers and hoped we could contact each other again. The next day Sunday, my new recruit invited me to come to his house for his son's birthday. There I met the wedding couple again. They happened to be friends with my new recruit. My recruit and I talked to the wedding couple and recruited them. My recruit got excited. From this couple, we started a recruiting frenzy. To this day, this leg accounts for about one third of my organization, including several big builders and hundreds of SMDs.

The recruiting habits of prospecting, approaching and dropping by pay dividends in building our future organization. Once you have a recruiting mentality, you think about recruiting everyday.

How can you tell whether a person has developed a recruiting mentality?

◆ *She always has a prospect list and a prospect book.* She looks at it everyday, adds more names and keeps it updated with follow ups. She also has her teammates do the same. She takes time to help a new recruit not only develop their prospect list but also quantify and qualify the names on that list. Prospect list is a major part of her team development. She holds training on prospect list and challenges people to constantly get more names.

◆ *She monitors her team's bubble chart regularly* and makes sure new recruits get a recruit under them as soon as possible. She matches up the new recruit and the trainer for recruiting. She asks them to invite guests to the BPM.

◆ *She believes recruiting solves all problems in the business.* She doesn't major in minor things. She knows the main thing is to recruit and build recruiting habits in her team.

◆ *She has a long-term goal for recruiting.* For example, getting her team to 100 recruits per month by the end of the year.

◆ *Most of her activity in the field are on recruiting* or fast starting a new recruit to get more recruits.

◆ *She drops by, stops by.* She creates a culture of prospecting and seeing people face to face. She increases contact and does more survey cards.

◆ *She organizes home BPMs* to increase invitations and presentations.

◆ *She believes in large numbers,* knowing that large numbers of activity are the key to break through to a recruiting explosion.

◆ *Her team believes they are always one recruit away from an explosion.*

◆ *She minimizes talk about the right or wrong market.* People may limit themselves or overreach toward certain types of people. She doesn't prejudge people. She's not impressed with so-called hot shots. She understands anyone can be big if they focus on activity and follow the system.

◆ *She's confident.* She doesn't cross recruit from other teams or other hierarchies. It would hurt her team in the long run. The ocean is big. There are plenty of fish for everyone.

◆ *She doesn't make a big deal about having people from the industry.* These people might have licenses and know other agents and clients, but they also have more problems following the system.

◆ *She accepts that she is in the recruiting and building business.* She overcomes her fear of prospecting and talking to people. Everyone she sees and meets is a potential recruit.

◆ *She consistently invites guests to the BPM,* has personal recruits every month and leads her team by example.

◆ *She is obsessed with recruiting,* and her team knows that. She's a recruiting woman, building a recruiting machine.

◆ *When running the system,* she knows the result of a good system is increasing the number of recruits, which will eventually increase sales, licenses and promotions.

◆ *She looks into her team's recruiting numbers and monitors them regularly.* She checks the leaders bulletin and knows she can compete with anyone if she has more recruits over a long period of time.

You must eat, sleep and breathe recruiting. You believe the best way to help team members is to build in them recruiting habits, to help them develop a recruiting mentality.

24

FAST START
MENTALITY

"Retain more people faster."

SPEED IS AN IMPORTANT PART OF OUR BUSINESS. I saw the business presentation on a Saturday morning, got excited right away and believed this was the business I had been looking for. But the minute I got home, my wife was the first one who showed doubt. And that weekend when I talked to everyone I came in contact with, no one seemed to support me or said good things about it. My enthusiasm dropped from level 10 to below zero. Luckily, my return interview was on Monday. My trainer was able to extinguish all the negativity I received. She revived my dream. I joined Monday and came back Tuesday with my wife to observe the presentation on the product and solutions. We loved what we saw. We became clients, believed in the product, and I went out in the field that night, having my first three field training presentations the second day in the business. I had a fast start.

Looking back, that was probably the best thing that could have happened to me. Within the first few days, all my doubts and fears were quickly resolved in the follow up interview, the product presentation and field training. I could see how we help people. The presentation was simple to understand and to duplicate. My confidence grew, and I became very proud about the business.

My wife also saw the goodness and the potential. Her approval was so important to me. The fast start saved me. I was recruited and retained.

Unfortunately, not all new recruits are as fortunate as I was. Imagine a parent has to leave the house to buy groceries. She tells her 19-year-old daughter to look after the baby. The 19-year-old then asks her 12-year-old brother to babysit. The boy in turn tells his 9-year-old sister to keep watch. Next thing they know the baby falls out of the bed.

The same lack of attention occurs in our business. We have the SMD, the MD, the Trainer, the Associate, the trainee and the new recruit. The SMD thinks the MD will take care of everything in his base. The MD assumes the Trainer looks after his team. The Associate thinks it is the job of his upline to know everything. The trainee brings in his friend, the new recruit. The trainee, of course, can't fast start his friend, and the new recruit may not listen to his friend anyway. The Associate doesn't have the ability to help. The Trainer doesn't have time. Many of them are part time and may not pay attention to all the new recruits joining the business. Most MDs assume the Trainer would do that job. Some MDs and SMDs also fear overlapping the Trainer. Sadly, the end result is many new recruits were not attended to and therefore not fast started early enough. They were left unprepared to deal with negative feedback from their friends and relatives. They were beaten up by the criticism and gave up on the business before giving it a shot.

The key element of fast start is the Trainer.
Like an air traffic controller, she must know every airplane appearing on her radar. For the system to work, the SMD, MD and Trainer must be on top of the situation. They must know immediately about any new recruits entering the base and assign a trainer to take care of the new recruit in the first 24 to 48 hours.

When you run the base, you must treat everyone like your direct recruit. You must take personal responsibility to ensure new recruits are fast started as soon as possible. Thus, you personally contact every new recruit, welcome them into your team and tell them you will take charge of getting them started. The best way is to set up a proper interview. During the interview, you will make a connection, answer questions and guide them to the next step.

The Trainer must come to the new recruit's home to meet the spouse. Meeting his wife or her husband is not only a key factor in our system but also necessary for the fast start. Fast start requires trust—trust from the new recruit and trust from the spouse. No person would allow their spouse to go out nightly with a stranger to do a new business they know nothing about. I was glad Hoa met my trainer the second day of the business, so when I went out to the field, she knew what we were doing.

There is magic in going to the new recruit's house. When they open the door and let you in, they take a big step to accept you into their lives. When you sit down with the spouse, it's critical that you share with them our mission and show your conviction about the business. If they see that we make a positive difference for families, you will get them all in. When they become a client, they believe in what we do. They join, they own and now they're ready to share and work with you.

"Fast start is retention. You have a great chance to keep the new recruit in the business once you fast start them."

Don't shortcut the fast start. Establishing a trustworthy relationship with the family will retain the new recruit and solidify our business. When new recruits feel good about the business, doing the prospect list is much easier and dropping by their top five closest friends and relatives within the first few days should be no problem. Once you got them fast started, you can get them to commit to the system, to recruit 3 people and observe 3 sales presentations in the first 30 days.

A lot of trainers complain about the lack of cooperation from the new recruit, particularly their unwillingness to do 3-3-30. I think it has a lot to do with whether they were properly fast started. A lot of leaders hope classroom training, the upstart program or orientation would do the job. Classes help but are not persuasive enough to move people. During my entire building career, I believed the fast start responsibility is in the hands of the Trainer. I can't remember a single time when a new recruit would ask the Trainer to take him out. I knew if I wanted to get him to fast start, I must come to his house and be the one to initiate.

DEVELOP A FAST START HABIT

◆ *Make a welcome call to the new recruit as soon as you can.* The new member would feel great to receive a call from the Trainer, the MD or the SMD.

◆ *Make appointment for a proper interview.*
During the interview, the Trainer and trainee
get the chance to know each other. The Trainer
listens to their dreams, goals and purpose for doing
the business.

◆ *Have a fast start kit* and make sure you go
through it and ask them to read it.

◆ *Come to the new recruit's home to meet the
spouse.* Get to know their family. Visualize your
friendship and business partnership prospering for
the long term.

◆ *Get them out in the field,* and with their
spouse if possible, to see their closest circle of
friends and relatives. These are the people they can
drop by, stop by comfortably at any time. The new
recruit needs to see a simple presentation, the good
work we do for families and the friendly manner
in which we conduct business. That will give them
confidence to move forward.

◆ *Fast start activity is more important than
results.* The recruits and sales will come. Thus, be
careful not to match up with a trainer who will just
focus on getting the sale.

◆ *Keep the fast start process simple, clear and fast.* A lengthy presentation or a long closing process may not be a good thing. If you get the sale, but the trainee sees it was too difficult and complicated, he won't see himself doing it.

Fast start is our system at work. People will understand the business much faster than with all the explanations, orientation or motivation. Don't just talk about it. Do it.

At the same time, be careful not to be too pushy. You can only fast start those who want to be fast started. For different reasons, some people can't fast start or are not ready. Respect their decision, hope for the best and keep encouraging them.

If you can't retain them through fast start, then retain them through slow start. Time and again, I've seen a lot of people do nothing in the first several months, and then one day something clicks. They change and start running. I want to be good at fast start, but I also want to be great at keeping people. The ability to retain people is one of the main reasons we are able to build a big team.

25

MEETING
MENTALITY

"The school of success."

F I HAD A MAGIC WAND, I WOULD MAKE OUR BUSINESS LIKE A SCHOOL where the students were required to attend classes and training and do field work for four years in order to graduate as an entrepreneur in the New Financial Industry. The rate of success would be astounding.

Deep in my heart, I strongly feel that anyone who brings that level of commitment to our business will achieve beyond their expectation. I believe our business can produce more success than other colleges with the same investment of time and effort. In the past 28 years, I witnessed many dedicated people become good students of the business. They've achieved impressive results for their effort. Many of them make good money part time. Quite a few make big money and go full time.

If you look into any new business, it takes at least two years for someone to understand it. Whether you open a restaurant, a flower shop or a tax service, the first two years are try, fail and try again. You learn when you do well, and you learn more when you mess up.

When I started the business, I loved the good things we stood for but hated the rejection everyday. I was told to attend the meeting every Tuesday night and

Saturday morning. I showed up. It was exciting and motivating at first. Around me were a lot of new people. They were very enthusiastic. They looked sharp, spoke professionally and came from good backgrounds. Inside, I felt they were better than me. I wondered if I had a chance. We attended upstart classes and understood this was a new business and there would be a long road ahead. Gradually, many people dropped out. Some complained. Some said they were too busy. Some came late. I soon realized I was one of the few who stayed. Every week we had new people come, and every week we had more people quit.

Then I recruited people. I thought they would do as I did, but they didn't. They followed the same pattern of slowly disappearing. Most just showed up to the meeting a handful of times. Few learned anything. They didn't give themselves a chance.

My fear of not being able to compete with them became unnecessary. The real fear was whether I would survive myself. Could I stay in the business? It didn't take long for me to figure out the reason why people fail. If I wanted to succeed, all I had to do is not do what they do. I also didn't need to be a rocket scientist to figure out that in a battle, if most fighters are out, the last one standing wins.

The big challenge in our business is our freedom. We can do it fast. We can do it slow. Or we can do nothing. The Trainer can advise, suggest and motivate. They can do everything except force people to show up. That's the problem. Most people don't attend the meeting. I was frustrated but understood. If every employer gives the employee the freedom not to show up but still get paid, few will go to work. If students aren't required to go to school, most won't attend. And if businesses don't have to be open and can still make money, the owner won't show up.

The secret of success in our business is how to get people to the meeting long enough to learn the business without demands or requirements. We should create a meeting mentality, a culture of learning, a habit of showing up.

◆ *Do it first.* Never miss a meeting.

◆ *When a new recruit joins,* spend time with him or her to discuss the importance of the meeting.

◆ *Treat it like a business.* Your store hours are Tuesday night and Saturday morning. As a business owner, you always show up.

◆ *Block your calendar on these days* and make sure your family knows this time is committed to the business.

◆ *Come early and stay late.* That's what businesspeople do.

◆ *Come to learn and participate.* Don't disturb or distract others.

◆ *Don't make appointments during meeting times.* It will erode your team's commitment to the meeting.

◆ *Volunteer to help and support during the meeting.* It's your on-the-job training.

◆ *Don't bring bad news or negativity to the meeting.* This is happy hour for the business.

◆ *Attend the Manager's Meeting.* Stay for the baseshop meeting.

◆ *Promote all meetings, local events and conventions.* This is the true sales skill of the builder.

◆ *Meetings build minds, move hearts and change lives.* You believe in the miracle of the meeting and event. Small meetings build small teams. Big events build big organizations.

◆ *No one can be built overnight,* but they are the products of everything they learned and felt during all the meetings and events over the years.

◆ *When looking for great builders,* don't pay too much attention to skills or talent. Look at their meeting behavior to see if they have the ability to build and lead an organization. You can recognize a big builder by looking at how many people follow him or her to a big event.

◆ *You can beat any person* by having more people attend the meeting and event.

◆ *A team who lacks a meeting mentality* is like an army whose soldiers don't show up to training camp. When you look for a strong team, look at the way the team shows up, how they perform at meetings and events. In a big convention, you can identify the strength, discipline and will to win of some teams as well as the weakness, disorganization and indifference of other teams.

◆ *In college, students who compete* come to class with a different attitude than others who just show up. Don't just go to the meeting. Come ready to win, to build something big, to be somebody.

◆ *Some builders lose their edge over time.* They act as if they know everything and do not sit in the meeting. They often hang around the back and chat with some important people. They think their team needs to sit, but not them. Most of these builders will not grow. They're making a fundamental mistake.

◆ *The meeting is the tough part of the business.* Lack of a meeting mentality reveals a lack of discipline. Undisciplined people have no hope to compete.

◆ *Monitor the number of your people at the meeting.* If the numbers drop, you're dying. If the number grows, you're winning. Count the people who show up twice a week and the people who never miss the meeting. That's the real number of people you have. The others are unpredictable people. They are like the weather—you never know.

For the past few years, we put incredible effort into building a meeting mentality. Our meetings are packed, our attendance has grown and our attitudes have risen. It's been a game changer. When we started the Manager's Meeting, only a handful of team members showed up. Now we have standing room only, not only in our office but across the country.

The meeting brings hope and confidence. People learn more, understand more and feel good about what we do.

THE SYSTEM WORKS, BUT ONLY WHEN PEOPLE SHOW UP AND GO TO WORK

When you have three people consistently going to the meeting, you start a small team. When you have five, you have a baseshop. You will likely get 5-5-30 and become a trainer. You will make good part-time income.

When you have 10 people committed to the meeting, you have a strong base. You may get 10-10-30, and you're on your way to build a big baseshop.

When you have 30 people with a meeting mentality, you will be in the big leagues, a major player on your way to becoming a World System Builder.

Building a meeting mentality is doable. You can do it. Your team can do it. You can build 3, 5, 10 and then 30 people. It's so easy to build when you have a meeting mentality, and your team duplicates it.

A teammate I'll call Renaissance came to Gold Street office with a handful of people. She was committed to the business and had big dreams, but things didn't seem to be working out. The office also had its own problems. We had good people but no unity. Lack of discipline was a major challenge. Full-timers showed up at BPM meetings but did not come to the office daily. The part-timers and sometimers were even worse. On the BPM night, lack of cooperation led to poor preparation. We recruited but couldn't retain people. Our spirit was low.

"Let other teams talk about complicated formulas and sophisticated products. Let them spend all their time fixing problems. You focus on the meeting. You systematically build a winning mentality."

I knew we needed someone who would rise up to make a change. Renaissance was the builder we had been looking for. She made a commitment to build a strong meeting mentality. She sold her house and moved closer to San Jose, so she could be at the office every day at 9am. She began to have her trainers meet early, so they could prepare for each day. Getting them on the same page was not an easy task since most of them did not have the habit of getting up early. Eventually, her persistence paid off. Those who showed up early started to grow.

I coached her to work on team attendance, promote the meeting and monitor the people who come to the BPM, especially the people who come twice a week. Attendance began to grow. At first, her team took up one row, then two rows, and soon her team reached more than 30 people. As predicted, she hit the green jacket and became CEO.

Our BPMs became packed. Other teams got excited. And everybody had confidence to win. Our Manager's Meeting also increased its participation. The full-timer, the Trainer and the builder all came.

I continually reminded the leaders about the importance of having a meeting mentality. Renaissance was doing well, but her team could be much better. One of her big legs had a major problem. He didn't show up at Tuesday Manager's Meetings. As a new SMD, he had no idea this would cost his team a great deal.

I asked him and his wife to see me. I told him how much I believed in him, in his potential and in his team's potential. But I didn't see how they would have a chance if he lacked the meeting discipline. I gave him an ultimatum. Either he showed up, or he had to find another office. He chose to stay and show up. Today, his team is exploding. He emerged as a great baseshop builder, became WSB and is now on his way to become a heavyweight contender. Renaissance also shot up like a rocket. Her team has the best meeting mentality. Every BPM night, her team attendance is as big as a mini convention.

26

TEAMWORK MENTALITY

*"A person's success depends on
how quickly he or she recognizes
we are in the team building business."*

WHEN PEOPLE JOIN, MOST ARE OVERWHELMED BY THE NEW BUSINESS. Fear and doubt preoccupy their minds. Afraid of being taken advantage of, they're unwilling to go out to the field from the get go. They'd rather be safe than sorry. Like a turtle hiding in its shell, they hold off and wait. They join the business but don't do the business.

Can we build these people? Yes, we can. If we can understand them and help them understand us, we can build together.

I was one of them. By the time most people come to our business they've been through a lot of hardship, failures, lay offs, debt and broken promises. In addition, the negative reaction from friends and relatives about our business increases their skepticism. In a world of doom and gloom, it's hard to be optimistic. Many can't pass through this fiery gate of doubt and distrust.

For those who make it through the early stages, the problems don't go away. Conflict with their leader, with the people in the office and especially with their team diminishes their belief in teamwork. Many end up engaging with other people's problems, a battle they can't win. They become withdrawn, protective, shielding, uncooperative and uncoachable. They complain that others are not team players, yet they themselves are not easy to work with. They're always right, while other people are wrong or misunderstand them.

Whether we recognize it or not, we are all part of a team. Our family is a team. If we are not team players, we will have a divided, broken family. When we go to school, work or social gatherings, we are also on a team. Some play an active part of this team effort; some are not that engaging. Some people will only be involved if something's in it for them. We've seen couples separate, friendships end, business partners fight, companies fail and countries collapse. The world is full of bad teams and doomed organizations.

> *"Teamwork is a rare commodity, not only in business but in all aspects of our lives. Teamwork is dream-work, and lack of it is a nightmare."*

To have teamwork, you have to work for it. It doesn't come naturally or by accident. Either you build up the team, or it will unravel. You should know how to build it, why it grows and why it dies. You should be a student of the team building business—what it takes to be a team player and what it takes to have a great team. Everyone wants to be a leader, but who wants to be a team player? The road to building a team is full of hazards and danger. Builders must face these challenges with determination, vision and a high level of tolerance.

In my early days, we were small. Though we had problems, they were mostly minor misunderstandings. As the team grew, bigger issues emerged. We could work hard to build up momentum, but just one guy throwing in a negative remark would defuse all the excitement. I felt as if he was always ready with a needle. As soon as the balloon started to inflate, he'd pop it. When we came to a decision, a few days later some people would do the opposite. Or when we created a contest, someone would compete unfairly, and the whole thing fell apart. Like building a house, the team business takes a long time to build up but little time to tear down.

People tend to stay together when small, but they change when they get bigger. You can see great teamwork during the growth phase, while most plateau phases are normally the result of fragmentation. Many builders break out too soon and can't grow due to isolation. When they run their own operation, they gain control, but they become the target of every arrow from their team.

They end up dealing with a lot of people problems and don't have people who support them.

Of course, in the people business, we have people problems. Either you control the problem, or the problem controls you. Don't let people problems affect the business, dim your vision and destroy team unity.

COMING TOGETHER AS A TEAM

◆ *First, we must come together.* There is no teamwork unless we show up. Going to the meeting is not only building a meeting mentality but the essential foundation for teamwork.

◆ *Keeping together is progress.* Avoid conflicts. There are two sides to every story. Don't just hold onto your position. You must hear the other side. Don't always jump in to defend your downline. They may be the cause of the problem. Remember: Most conflicts may not be important. Don't spend your time solving problems no one will remember 30 days from now. An elder once told me about the daily squabbles he had with his wife. The older he got, the less he remembers any of it.

◆ *When dealing with people, you don't really win when you win.* And you don't necessary lose when you back down or let them feel they are winning. The real win is when your team wins. If you lose and the team wins, did you lose? But if you win and the team loses, who is the loser?

◆ *You don't need to like each other to work together.* All the store owners in a shopping mall may not get along individually, but they always show up and open their store everyday. All you need is a common vision and a commitment to build for the success of the entire team.

WHO CARES?

Every team needs players who put the team first. The number one ingredient of teamwork is care. If you don't care, you don't have a team. Team members must know each one of them is critical for the success of the team, and the success of the team is the success of each individual.

When you care, you show up to the meeting. You don't want to make your leader worry. You don't want your people disappointed. You cheer people up, defuse conflict and promote friendship. When you care, you want to perform. You want your leader to win, to get to the top. You know when your leader wins, then the team wins and you win too. You want to be part of a winning team. If you don't care whether or not the team wins, you have a serious teamwork problem, and you may find building your own team a hard thing to do.

◆ *As a builder, put your teammate first.* When you deal with your team, make sure they always get the better end of the deal. Don't be fair to them. Be more than fair to your people. When your team looks at you, they should have confidence in your commitment. They don't worry about your integrity, and most importantly they know you care.

◆ *Treat people well. Know your people.* Know their dreams, their goals and their purpose. Know the difficult situations they have. Help them overcome their challenges or stand by them when they need you.

◆ *Know their family.* When you care for their family, you are part of their family. Invite them to your home to meet your family, and treat them like family.

◆ *Hold team events and gatherings.* Help the team get to know each other. Also get their families involved.

◆ *Be a friend first. Then be a leader.* Some people say friendship and leadership don't mix. In our business it works quite well. We are not a traditional employer/employee business. We are partners in a team building business. We don't work for—we work with one another.

Teamwork allows us to have bigger vision. If you want to build it big, not only must you be a big leader, you must also be a bigger team player. This is not an easy task. Those who don't know a lot speak a lot. And those who don't speak a lot know a lot. Those who show don't have. And those who have don't show. Great leaders don't take credit. They're great by bringing out the best in people, and pushing their people up. A great leader is smaller than the team. And a small leader is bigger than the team.

> *"Take care of your people, and your people will take care of you. When people work together, success will take care of itself."*

Teamwork is powerful and contagious. Once a group of people has a teamwork mentality, they shoot for the stars. When teamwork is your habit, you bring support, happiness and a winning attitude to people around you.

CAN YOU BUILD A BUILDER'S MINDSET?

The bad news is it will be hard and take a long time. Getting into a small habit like walking a few miles a day or being on time are still not easy. Imagine trying to build a recruiting mentality, a fast start mentality, a meeting mentality and a teamwork mentality. It will be a long road.

The good news is you don't have to be perfect. You don't even have to wait long to see the benefits. For example, if you want to be a bodybuilder, you don't have to wait until you have a perfect body to call it a success. You can feel the benefits quickly. You are stronger, healthier and more energetic.

To build a builder's mind, first recognize its importance and make a decision to become a System Builder. When you start a new habit, it will be awkward and uncomfortable in the beginning. But give yourself a chance.

See yourself as the luckiest person on earth. I do. I picture myself a fortunate man. I'm here in the land of the free. I become an entrepeneur. I set my own schedule. I can build as big as I want. I'm so privileged to be part of a major movement, building a new industry, changing my life and changing people's lives. I see myself joining a championship team, playing the most important game of my life.

I look at builders, present and past. I think they are the greatest people. They come to this earth, building, contributing and making the world a better place. They build schools, churches, roads, bridges, cities and nations. They build machines, cars, ships and computers.

We build people. We help people fulfill their potential and become their best, by doing their best. Builders look for challenges and conquer them. Bigger builders want bigger challenges.

Enjoy the process. Every time I go to the meeting, I feel as if I'm seeing my friends. Every time I go out in the field, I meet new friends. Every time we sit down with people, what a wonderful experience!

You must love something so much to do something you hate so much. Like athletes pushing themselves to their physical limits or the explorer enduring long stretches of loneliness, we are a different breed, doing things most people wouldn't want to do.

Develop a positive attitude to build. Enthuse yourself by recruiting. Be excited in the fast start.

Enjoy the meeting and love the teamwork. See
the glass as half full, not half empty. In the people
business, people will certainly bring you a lot of
people problems, but they will also bring you
inspiration, success and achievement beyond your
imagination.

You may make good money and acquire fancy
items, but few things can compare to the joy of
winning, when you know you can do it, when you
do your best and you bring out the best in you. Like
a devoted climber reaching the top of the mountain,
looking up, only you and the sky, the struggle and
pain you endured is worth all the effort.

27

SELLING THE DREAM OR SELLING THE BUSINESS?

"Selling the dream business."

WHEN I JOINED THE BUSINESS, I WAS LIKE A PERSON WHO LIVED IN A BLACK AND WHITE MOVIE, AND ALL OF A SUDDEN I SAW IN TECHNICOLOR. The excitement, the environment and the motivation were so incredible. People clapped, cheered and chanted as if it was a carnival. I was overwhelmed and intimidated. A good part of me liked it, but the other part felt uneasy. I had mixed feelings. Sometimes I was attracted to this new environment; sometimes I was turned off. I felt the same way the first time I put on skis and started going down the mountain. I was excited to experience something new but was a little afraid and definitely uncomfortable.

Personally, I wanted my trainers to tell me more about the business—how it works, how to make money, how good the product is and how to build an organization. But what I mostly heard were personal stories and motivational speeches. I eventually got used to it and became part of the dream selling business.

In fact, that was the purpose. On a typical BPM night, all they did was sell the dream. Sell the dream to the new prospect in the BPM. Resell the dream to the current team member. And teach the team how to sell the dream.

Selling the dream is in our blood. We have brochures, flyers and magazines that flaunt successful people living in beautiful houses, driving fancy cars and going on luxury trips. At our meetings and conventions, we show pictures of the many blessings of this business. We practice showing off and are getting good at it. We eat, sleep, talk and sell the dream. It works. Many of us have become very successful. We sell the dream, and our dreams come true. If it's not broke, why fix it?

WHAT IS THE DREAM?

I met a woman in Central Vietnam. Born handicapped, she was abandoned at birth and lived on the streets. She survived by doing labor for street vendors her entire life. A nun found her in her late 50's and brought her to a convent where we met. I never saw a happier woman. She smiled all the time and kept saying, "I'm so happy. I'm in heaven!" For the first time in her life, she had food, a bed and her own room.

When I was a social worker, we resettled many veterans from the Vietnam War. Some soldiers were in the reeducation camp for so long they sometimes pinched themselves in the middle of the night to make sure they were not in jail anymore.

On the other hand, in the world of the rich and famous, quite a few are living a nightmare. They have everything but live in misery. They use drugs to escape to another world, and some never wake up.

Are you living your dream, or are you facing your nightmare? Dreams and nightmares are part of our life, but most of us don't pay attention to them. We just let them go in any direction. I was lucky I had a chance to recognize my dream, work to make it a reality and direct it toward the future I desired.

THE IMPORTANCE OF SELLING THE DREAM

The purpose of selling the dream is to make people believe in their dreams. Eleanor Roosevelt proclaimed, "The future belongs to those who believe in the beauty of their dreams." I believe in my dreams, and it helps me last through tough times.

Dream and fear are archenemies. If your dream is strong enough, it'll overcome your fear. But if your fear is so big, it will kill your dream. Most men and women grow up dreamers. They all want to be successful and fulfill their dream. In the land of opportunity, the shining star of the free enterprise system, most people give up on their dream and live a life of quiet desperation. In fact, they never try, and if they do, they give up so easily. The main reason is their fear is much bigger than their dream.

That's why we must be able to dream again. That's why we need to sell the dream, and they need to buy the dream. Without people who dare to dream, we would not have built spaceships, and astronauts would not have landed on the moon. We are an organization of dreamers, people who conquer our fear to pursue our dream. The reason we can do this is because we are together. We sell the dream to each other. We encourage the weak. We praise the strong. And we win the battle over fear. When you are alone, your dream is fragile. But when dreamers are together, they can move mountains.

Fundamentally, selling the dream is bringing good news and sharing good things. We bring fresh water to the thirsty. As for me, I'm more than thirsty. I'm in a long drought. Our modern time is full of traffic, work, bills, bad news and obligations. We are always busy and stressed out. I wanted some good news, and we have great news here.

Some of us don't recognize the power of our system. We build a dream business. We build a system where dreaming never stops. Any organization, especially the people in our industry, won't be able to grow or sustain growth unless they can capture the dreaming power of their field force. If they can build a dream machine, sell a real dream and capture the heart and soul of their people, they can build a team as big as their dream.

The industry can't compete with this powerful model. Even though they have agents working full time, selling product is the only thing they do. They won't be able to grow. These salesmen are living their nightmare of quotas, of not hitting the deadline, of not being able to get the commission. If they don't sell, they don't eat.

HOW TO SELL THE DREAM

There are two types of dream selling. The first is to sell the business, and the second is to sell the dream to become somebody. Many of our teammates cannot see the difference and make major mistakes in this area.

Let's keep it simple:

◆ *You sell the business to recruit.*

◆ *You sell the dream to retain.*

You serve food to the hungry and water to the thirsty, not the other way around. The mix up can cost you the recruit, and you may fail to keep your people.

SELL THE BUSINESS DREAM

You must totally sell out to your business. If you know why it is the best business in the world, then you are ready to sell the dream of joining this dream business. That is why in the early days you should go out with a trainer, someone who knows how to sell the business. Your excitement and your relationship with the prospect helps, but you need the Trainer to sell the good qualities of our business.

If you show people the trips and the big money, but the prospect wants to know about the winning strategies of our business and why we're better than the rest, you're serving water to the hungry. Selling the dream instead of selling the business won't deliver results. You might impress but won't convince. Early on, the new recruit prefers to learn about the products, the system and our advantages. If all they see is selling the dream, you won't give them enough confidence in the business to stay.

When people buy into your business, sell them the business. Imagine you sell McDonald's franchises.

The prospect wants to know more about the business deal, the training, the operation, the revenues and the costs. But all they hear from you is selling the dream to be somebody. When a business is proven, you don't have to sell the dream. You sell the business. You sell the reasons for its success: better product, better service and better support.

BE GOOD AT SELLING YOUR BUSINESS

◆ *The vision of the business*

◆ *The mission of the business*

◆ *The system of the business*

Sell the big dream of our business. People won't be part of a small dream.

Our Vision is to build a New Industry to replace the old, outdated industry. We want to build the largest distribution system in the financial industry. We're growing, and they're shrinking.

We have a big Mission to help people build a strong financial foundation to achieve financial independence. We want to help solve the consumer's dilemma—lack of understanding, planning and support. We want to fix the retirement crisis and the growing financial problems that hurt our families and our country.

We sell a revolutionary System, the solution for building a big business. Millions of people are looking for a good business model that they can believe in, that is real and honest, that brings value to the family and yet is doable for them to invest their effort into. People are tired of empty promises. They want a solid industry, something that will last, and a proven system they can build on.

SELLING YOUR DREAM

Sell your dream. But sell their dream too. If they dream of a piece of pie, and you give them salad, it won't go well. People will follow their dream, not your dream. Make sure you make the right connection.

You attract people based on what you sell, so be careful in the selling of big income, houses, cars or other material things. Money is a good incentive but not always and sometimes not enough. We have people who join because of reasons other than money. When I started, I heard my leader say the people who joined for the money won't last long enough to make money. I found that quite ironic.

I did join for the money. I wanted to make extra income and a lot more if possible. But I later found out it wasn't just about the money. It was what I wanted to do with the money. I wanted to pay off my debt, make enough income for my wife to stay home, provide my children a better education and take care of our parents. Those were the reasons for the money. Without a strong reason, people won't have the commitment and endurance to last.

Thus, selling income without a good reason is not good enough. Every time I sit down with a teammate, if she shares with me her top 10 reasons why she does the business, and those reasons are more than about her own personal desires, I know she bought the dream. People will endure and fight much harder for their loved ones than for themselves. However, if the top reasons are all the material stuff, I'm not sure she will last. This business, as with most businesses, is very tough in the early stages. Only the people with strong conviction will persevere.

WHAT WE OFFER

The market changed greatly over the last 30 years. What we sold in the past may not be so appealing in the present or the future. Besides money, do we have more important things we can offer people?

The big selling point of the first company I joined was the crusade. We were fighting to correct some wrong. Thirty years ago, the Baby Boomers were young. They needed protection. We wanted to change the world and protect families. By the 1990's, more people were concerned about the investment equation and saving for retirement. This was the glitzy era of big houses and nice cars. But reality came with the 21st century. The stockmarket tanked. The housing market collapsed. People are now more cautious. They don't believe in quick and artificial but more on long term and real. Unfortunately, most companies in the industry haven't changed much. Old habits die hard. Most of them still practice the same things they did 20, 30 years ago.

On the other hand, we have many great things to sell.

◆ *To be somebody.*

The fact that you are on your way to become the person you want to be is a big deal. I'm passionate about my business. I sell this thing all the time. Although I had a lot of childhood struggles and felt inferior due to my humble background, my confidence grew. My ability to communicate improved. And I was able to provide for my family. These are my best selling points. I found that my growth in becoming somebody was more important than the money I made. Because of this, I was able to connect with potential prospects much better than dazzle them with my income.

Deep down, most people are trapped. They don't like the situation they're in. They don't feel good about themselves. And they want to be somebody. When they see someone like yourself who was able to work your way out of your challenges, they think this can be something very worth looking into. The sparkle in your eye, the passion in your voice and the seriousness of your body language will sell the dream better than your title or your income.

◆ To provide for my family.

I try not to show off what I have. Rather I focus more on what my family receives. I don't have to tell people about my income. They see what I can do for my family, not just for my wife and kids but for all the people around me. That is important to me. You'll attract people who care for the family. We are a family-based business.

◆ *Sell freedom.*

I'm in business. I'm my own boss and call my own shots. Every time I talk about it, I'm so happy. I want to work hard but not for someone else. I make a compelling point on the beauty of our freedom.

We don't have a boss or a manager. We have business partners. We also don't boss anybody around. We have no quotas nor deadlines. We set our own goals. We can do nothing, or we can be as big as we want—no ceiling, no income restrictions, no territory limits.

◆ *Sell integrity.*

We help people. We bring them in, teach them, train them and don't ask or demand from them anything. They don't have to buy anything. If they own the product, it's because they need it and want it. I am so proud of this fact. The integrity of our system is unmatched in the business world. Sell integrity. Sell the clean and clear way of our business.

◆ *Sell security.*

Most people don't recognize the wonderful advantage of our business is the security for the long term. Income streams from overrides, supervision, renewals and trails are the income security we have. I know money is important. Most people work for money, but more want the security.

◆ *Conviction to contribute.*

We can make the world a better place. We bring trust back to a doubtful world and teamwork to lonely businesspeople. We create fun and happiness with family events and trips that bond us together. Rather than perpetuate the boss/employee order, we bring respect in working relationships. We have a better way to build the business.

◆ *Sell your success.*

There is nothing wrong with buying a big house and your dream car and enjoying a wonderful life. You earned it. You should enjoy it. You should experience the best of the best, do things few can do and go places few people go. I'm not against having fun and living a good life. In fact, I like to do so myself.

LIVING THE DREAM OR SELLING THE DREAM?

I made a big shift in my understanding about selling the dream some time ago. I found living the dream is the best way to sell the dream. People are like their shadows. When you chase it, it runs away.

But when you walk away, it follows you. The more I sell the dream, the more people doubt. Some even ask directly, "If it's so good, why do you need to sell that hard?" The more I sell that we can make big money, the more they question if it's real. The more we show off the car and the house, they think we bought it for business purposes.

When I started, what I was most afraid of was when people asked me how much money I made. I had to explain I just started and will eventually make money. They told me, "Why don't you go ahead and make that money, then come back and see me!" When I told them I hit six-figures and showed them the ring, they asked for more proof!

Eventually I sent my kids to private schools, let my wife stay at home, moved to a bigger office and hired more staff to work for me. People began to pay attention.

I live my dream every day. Every time I walk in the office and into a meeting, I'm on cloud nine. I'm so happy to be in the business. I don't have to make big money to sell the dream because I'm living the dream now. I'm in a dream business with a great vision, a big mission and a proven system. I'm like a person who just started the most successful franchise.

I'm on my way to become somebody. I provide for my family. I have freedom to do the business.
I am so proud of the security, the integrity and the contribution we make to society. The prospect can see it. The team can feel it.

DO WHAT YOU LOVE

It's not a cliché. Do what you love. Don't say what you love. Doing what you love is truly what it means to sell the dream. People like Mother Theresa, Muhammad Ali and Steve Jobs sold the dream to people better than anybody because they just did what they loved.

Instead of selling our people dream trips, we brought them to those destinations. We brought thousands of people to Hawaii, the Caribbean, Asia and Europe. We don't need to sell the dream. Our people live the dream. Their children and their parents live the dream. The world out there is full of organizations where a few get to sell the dream to the many. We move to the next level. We all live the dream together.

And the journey will be continued...

Books by Xuan Nguyen

◆ *The System Builder, Fourth Edition*
   $15.00, 341 pages

◆ *The System Builder Audiobook*
   $10.00, 6 Audio CDs, unabridged

◆ *The Moment of Truth: Facing the Challenges*
   $2.00, 40 pages

◆ *Building People: The Journey of a Builder 2.0*
   $5.00, 249 pages